NAVIGATING THE CORE

CURRICULUM

RTI Strategies to Support Every Learner

TOBY J. KARTEN

Solution Tree | Press

a division of
Solution Tree

555 North Morton Street
Bloomington, IN 47404
800.733.6786 (toll free) / 812.336.7700
FAX: 812.336.7790

email: info@SolutionTree.com
SolutionTree.com

Visit **go.SolutionTree.com/RTI** to download the free reproducibles in this book.

Printed in the United States of America

21   20   19   18   17   1   2   3   4   5

Names: Karten, Toby J., author.

Title: Navigating the core curriculum : RTI strategies to support every

learner / Toby J. Karten.

Description: Bloomington, IN : Solution Tree Press, 2017. | Includes

bibliographical references and index.

Identifiers: LCCN 2016055709 | ISBN 9781943874613 (perfect bound)

Subjects: LCSH: Response to intervention (Learning disabled children)--United

States. | Children with disabilities--Education--United States.

Classification: LCC LC4705 .K368 2017 | DDC 371.9--dc23 LC record available at https://lccn.loc.gov/2016055709

Solution Tree
Jeffrey C. Jones, CEO
Edmund M. Ackerman, President

Solution Tree Press
President and Publisher: Douglas M. Rife
Editorial Director: Sarah Payne-Mills
Managing Production Editor: Caroline Weiss
Senior Production Editor: Christine Hood
Senior Editor: Amy Rubenstein
Copy Editor: Ashante K. Thomas
Proofreader: Elisabeth Abrams
Text and Cover Designer: Abigail Bowen
Editorial Assistants: Jessi Finn and Kendra Slayton

This book is dedicated to my first teachers, my mother and father. My mother was a role model who persevered, despite the cards she was dealt; while my father taught me that compassion always endures. As loving facilitators, they structured my life. Time marches on, but solid core foundations shape future strides.

ACKNOWLEDGMENTS

I would like to acknowledge Douglas Rife for his collaboration. And yes, Philadelphia has the best cheese steaks and inviting places to begin conversations. Appreciation also goes to Amy Rubenstein, Christine Hood, and the Solution Tree staff for their assistance during this resource's preparation. And last but not least, thank you to my colleagues and students across the United States. You continually plan, intervene, instruct, learn, assess, collaborate, and still smile! Kudos to all of you—stay the course.

Solution Tree Press would like to thank the following reviewers:

Mary Anderson
RTI Specialist
Tavola Elementary School
New Caney, Texas

Kristie Bleers
RTI Facilitator
East Aurora School District 131
Aurora, Illinois

Visit **go.SolutionTree.com/RTI** to download the free reproducibles in this book.

TABLE OF CONTENTS

Reproducible pages are in italics.

ABOUT THE AUTHOR. xiii

INTRODUCTION 1
   Response to Intervention 1
      Systematic and Explicit Instruction. 3
      The Four Cs of RTI. 4
      Core Knowledge 5
   Structure of This Book 5

CHAPTER 1

OPENING DOORS FOR ALL LEARNERS 9

   RTI Variables 9
      Classroom Dynamics. 10
      Teacher Expertise 11
   Evidence-Based Practice 12
      Cohesive Framework. 12
      Prescriptive and Responsive Instruction 12
      Contextually Engaging Tasks. 14
   Multiple Curriculum Entry Points. 15
      Successful Strategies and Mindsets 15
      MTSS Lesson Connections 15
   Conclusion 17

CHAPTER 2

APPROACHING THE CORE VOCABULARY 19

Academic Language. 19

    Identify Vocabulary for Students With and Without IEPs 20

    Determine Student Levels 21

    Select Appropriate Interventions 21

Evidence-Based Practice 22

    Vocabulary Instruction 22

    Early Literacy Skills. 22

Multiple Curriculum Entry Points. 23

    How to Identify Knowledge, Intervene, and Ensure Internalization. . . . 24

    MTSS Lesson Connections 25

Conclusion 34

Phonemic Awareness and Fluency Record 35

Comprehension of Fiction, Narrative, and Expository Text. 36

A–Z Vocabulary List 37

PRO-Vocabulary Instruction 38

CHAPTER 3

CREATING TIERED INTERVENTIONS FOR LITERACY AND MATHEMATICS. 39

The Spectrum 40

    Academic Levels 41

    Interests 41

    Motivation 43

Evidence-Based Practice 44

    RTI-MTSS 44

    Differentiated Instruction 50

    Universal Design for Learning 51

Multiple Curriculum Entry Points. 52

    Step-by-Step Task Analysis 52

    MTSS Lesson Connections 52

    Overlearning and Automaticity. 57

Conclusion 58

Interests and Strengths Questionnaire. *59*

Tiered UDL-MTSS Literacy Planner *60*

Lesson-Planning Template: Learner Outcomes and Skills *62*

CHAPTER 4

IMPLEMENTING BEST PRACTICES 65

The Big Ideas. 66

    Literacy and Mathematics Achievements 66

    Interventions, Accommodations, and Modifications. 67

    Multitiered System of Supports 69

Evidence-Based Practice 69

    Strategic Reading and Writing Fluency 70

    Learning Environments 73

    Behavior. 74

    Assessment Data. 76

Multiple Curriculum Entry Points. 78

    MTSS Lesson Connections 78

    Learner Outcomes 80

Conclusion 84

Parts of a Book *86*

Syllable Types. *87*

Words and Questions Chart. *88*

People, Places, and Things Chart. *89*

Record of Mathematics Skills, Concepts, and Engagements. *90*

Record of Student Participation *91*

Reading Reflection Chart. *92*

Written Expression Chart *93*

Lesson-Planning Template: Lessons Across the Disciplines *94*

Curriculum Dice Game *95*

CHAPTER 5

OFFERING ACADEMIC AND BEHAVIORAL SUPPORT . . . 97

Respect for Learner Variability 98

Student-Specific Tiers 98

Collaborative Problem-Solving Approach 99

Evidence-Based Practice 100

Support for Academic Achievements 100

Positive Behavior Interventions and Supports 100

Attention and Cooperation 102

Multiple Curriculum Entry Points 103

Visual, Auditory, and Kinesthetic/Tactile Approaches 103

MTSS Lesson Connections 104

Conclusion 109

My Behavior Chart 111

Problem-Solving Approach: Turning Challenge Into Growth 112

CHAPTER 6

MINIMIZING AND MAXIMIZING STRATEGIC ENGAGEMENTS FOR RIGOROUS LEARNING 113

Challenge and Engage 114

Minimize and Maximize 114

Pace, Repeat, and Enrich 116

Fine-Tune and Individualize 120

Evidence-Based Practice 120

Cognitive Strategy Instruction 121

Triarchic Theory of Intelligence 121

Direct Instruction 122

Cooperative Learning 122

Peer Supports 124

Multiple Curriculum Entry Points 124

Real-World Connections 124

Strategic Engagements 125

Conclusion 130

KWL Chart 131

Quarterly Lesson Planner 132

Long-Range Monthly Planner 133

CHAPTER 7

ENSURING PROFESSIONAL FIDELITY 135

Professional Development 136

Preparation and Sustainability 139

Conclusion 140

Parameters for Professional Development. *141*

EPILOGUE

EMBRACING RTI 143

REFERENCES AND RESOURCES 145

INDEX 167

ABOUT THE AUTHOR

Toby J. Karten, a staff developer, instructional coach, educational consultant, author, and inclusion specialist, has taught learners ranging from preschool to graduate school. She is an adjunct professor with Monmouth University, College of New Jersey, and La Salle University. In addition, Toby has designed online courses and professional development units for pre-service and practicing educators and related staff for the Regional Training Center in Randolph, New Jersey, and online platforms across the United States.

She has collaborated with administrators, staff, students, and their families to ensure that students are educated in their least restrictive environments, looking at inclusive placements as the first option of service with the specially designed interventions in place.

Throughout her professional career, Toby has helped staff translate research into practical applications for preK–12 classrooms. She has spoken with and coached administrators, staff, students, and their families at local, national, and international school sites and educational conferences. Toby's ongoing professional goal is to help learners to achieve successful inclusion experiences in schools and ultimately, in life.

The Council for Exceptional Children and the New Jersey Department of Education recognized Toby as an exemplary educator, giving her two Teacher of the Year awards. She earned a bachelor of arts degree in special education from Brooklyn College, a master of science degree in special education from the College of Staten Island, a supervisory degree from Georgian Court University, and an honorary doctorate degree from Gratz College.

To learn more about Toby's work, visit her website at www.inclusionworkshops.com and follow @TJK2INCLUDE on Twitter.

To book Toby J. Karten for professional development, contact pd@SolutionTree.com.

INTRODUCTION

Before we arrive at a destination, we need to make a few decisions about our journey. We might know where we want to go, but first we need to accurately analyze the facts. Analysis takes into account the starting point, travel options, and time parameters. For example, one may be able to walk or board a train, bus, plane, or car to get to a given city. However, some modes of transportation are preferable over others; each choice has both benefits and disadvantages. If there is traffic on a road, then traversing on foot for five blocks is quicker than sitting in bumper-to-bumper traffic in a taxi. I often print a map, use a phone app, consult a friend, or look for directions online. Navigation requires planning, knowledge, step-by-step procedures, resources, collaboration, and then, after arrival, a review on whether the travel choice was a good one.

> *We might know where we want to go, but first we need to accurately analyze the facts.*

Schools are faced with similar decisions as they navigate their curriculum to assist or accompany their diverse learners to safely and happily arrive at their learning destinations. As an educator, instructional coach, and author, my goal for writing this book is to offer evidence-based "travel options" that will ease teachers' pedagogical journey for schools and their classrooms.

Response to Intervention

Teachers can use instructional tiers to help students who do not begin their journey at the same starting points. Diversity mandates that instructional decisions respond to multiple learner levels; this assists teachers in determining the best teaching approaches to reach each student. Ultimately, teachers must consider that learners are often at different levels of content mastery, even if they're in the same classroom. The response to intervention (RTI) approach addresses these levels.

RTI is a multitiered system of supports (MTSS) that offers diverse routes and step-by-step approaches such as differentiated instruction and universal design for learning (UDL) to help learners achieve mastery. RTI and MTSS are not separate ideas or concepts but partners that value how the core instruction is delivered to learners. Multitiered instruction is basically an instructional interaction. It is how teachers deliver the core instruction to students who learn differently. If teachers introduce, remediate, and enrich student levels with the whole class, small groups, and individuals, then they can effectively address student diversity.

RTI is often delivered in three tiers, as shown in figure I.1.

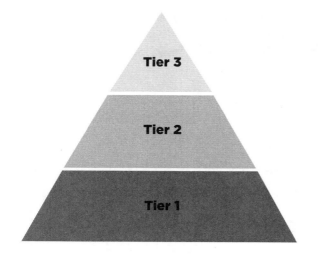

Source: Buffum, Mattos, & Weber, 2012.

Figure I.1: The traditional RTI pyramid.

According to Austin Buffum, Mike Mattos, and Chris Weber (2012):

> The pyramid shape is wide at the bottom to represent the basic instruction that all students receive. As students demonstrate the need for additional support, they move up the pyramid, receiving increasingly more targeted and intensive help. Fewer students should need the services offered at the upper levels, thus creating the tapered shape of a pyramid. The pyramid is also traditionally separated into tiers, with Tier 1 representing grade-level core instruction, Tier 2 supplemental interventions, and Tier 3 intensive student support. (p. 11)

Tier 1 instruction is for the whole class or small groups; not all learners master the learning initially. Tier 2 intervention provides supplemental instruction in small groups, as needed; and Tier 3 intervention provides instruction for individual students who require additional scaffolding and practice. To further reinforce this concept, Buffum and colleagues (2012) provide an inverted pyramid, which focuses on "a school's collective attention and resources to a single point: the individual child" (p. 11). The foundation for RTI is that schools should not delay helping struggling students until they fall so far behind that they then qualify for special education, but instead "should provide timely, targeted, systematic interventions to all students who demonstrate the need" (p. xiii). See figure I.2.

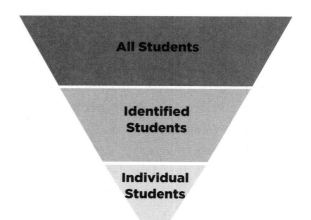

Source: Buffum et al., 2012.

Figure I.2: The inverted RTI pyramid.

They contend that the pyramid "should be wide at the top to represent access to the core grade-level curriculum that all students deserve and need" (p. 11). This initial core instruction should meet the needs of most students and embrace differentiation. However, beyond initial instruction, some students may need more focused, targeted instruction, and the school should respond by individually attending to the needs of each of these students.

Instruction can address oral expression, listening comprehension, early literacy skills, reading fluency, reading comprehension, vocabulary development, written expression, mathematical computations, mathematical problem solving, and critical-thinking skills across the grades and disciplines to help learners achieve academic success. Instruction and assistance to know and display appropriate behavioral, social, and emotional skills are also essential.

RTI requires teachers to provide systematic and explicit instruction to be sure they are planning, organizing, and sequencing their instruction in a way that makes sense to students at all levels of learning.

The following sections detail systematic and explicit instruction and how teachers can strategically implement it into the three tiers. You also will read about the four Cs of RTI, which identify the four guiding principles all educators should follow to help students succeed.

Systematic and Explicit Instruction

Systematic instruction is similar to a builder's blueprint for a house that is planned for and designed before building materials are gathered and construction begins (Colorado Department of Education, 2008). Even though systematic instruction refers to a carefully planned sequence for instruction, that does not translate to all heads facing forward using the same strategy at the same time for each student (Florida Department of Education, n.d.). Tiered instruction offers multiple entry points to allow students at varying levels to gain and retain knowledge and skills.

Explicit instruction requires strategic planning that links and builds on prior learning. Teachers must consider what students were taught, what students remember and can apply, and what students need to be taught. Multitiered instruction bridges gaps and connects students to newer concepts as the curriculum increases in complexity. Breaking up the learning into its discrete steps allows for practice, application, and retention within a multitiered approach.

Explicit instruction offers a road map for how a skill is taught, including a description of each step and the strategies employed. Concepts and skills to explicitly and systematically teach include phonemic awareness, phonics, vocabulary, fluency, comprehension, mathematics, and behavior. Vigilance with structure and then flexibility allow tiered instruction to be responsive to student needs, interests, and levels.

> *Teachers must consider what students were taught, what students remember and can apply, and what students need to be taught.*

Tier 1

Curriculum maps and lesson plans outline the core instruction, but they are never scripted ones, since student responses drive the choice of instructional programs and academic engagements. Tier 1 core instruction provides explicit evidence-based lessons for phonological segmentation, fluency, comprehension, basic mathematics facts, fractions, geometry, and algebra, to name a few academic areas, as well as monitoring on-task behavior to increase motivation and attention. Continual progress monitoring occurs throughout all of the tiers.

Responsive tweaking of instruction is based on student performance. Many teachers say they have experienced a scheduled fifty-minute period of instruction that some students grasp in fifteen minutes, while other students require fifty minutes or even five hours of instruction. Tier 1 often identifies the students who require additional instructional approaches to be given in Tiers 2 and 3.

Tier 2

Daniel Hallahan, James Kauffman, and Paige Pullen (2015) explain that Tier 2 usually takes about six to eight weeks. This time period allows students ample time to learn and then practice the skills. However, if a student is not showing any progress, six to eight weeks may not be realistic. Rollanda O'Connor and Janette Klingner (2010) state "the effectiveness of successful tiers depends not just on instructional content, but also on teachers' responsiveness to students who respond poorly, or, in other words, on teachers' instructional savvy and flexibility" (p. 303).

Tier 2 includes, but is not limited to, small-group instruction, multiple interventions and resources, increased feedback and monitoring, access to both grade-level and student-level text, frontloading the content and challenging vocabulary, and using companion materials that align with the core materials (National Center on Intensive Intervention at American Institutes for Research [AIR], 2014).

Tier 3

Academic and behavioral interventions are more individualized in Tier 3 for students with increased learning needs and challenging behaviors. These students often require prerequisite skills that allow them to achieve successful experiences with the core instruction. Increased monitoring and reinforcement offer students in Tier 3 alternate ways to achieve successful engagement with the academics as well as necessary self-reflection.

Skilled interventionists often provide instruction in Tier 3 within and outside the general education classroom to address students' skill deficits. Students may tap out syllables, practice multidigit computations, read and listen to appropriately leveled text to understand what is implied in a nonfiction article, and receive more intensive strategies to successfully experience learning and behavioral strides. Progress monitoring is more frequent in Tier 3, with heightened teacher and student reflections and increased collaborative planning.

The Four Cs of RTI

Buffum and colleagues (2012) refer to the four Cs of RTI, or the four practices all educators must follow if students are to succeed. They consider these the essential guiding principles of RTI.

1. **Collective responsibility:** Embraces the idea that the primary responsibility of each educator is to ensure high levels of learning for every student

2. **Concentrated instruction:** Is a systematic process of identifying essential knowledge and skills that all students must learn at high levels. This includes determining the specific learning needs for each student

3. **Convergent assessment:** Is a continual process of analyzing evidence to identify the specific learning needs for each student and the effectiveness of instruction in meeting those needs

4. **Certain access:** Is a process that ensures that every student receives the time and support needed to learn at high levels

These principles support learning the core as well as meeting national and provincial learning standards. At the writing of this book, education focuses on using national and provincial standards and narrowing the global achievement gap (Achieve, 2015). Preparing students for successful adult lives and to be college and career ready involves planning, communication, and collaboration.

Preparing students for successful adult lives and to be college and career ready involves planning, communication, and collaboration.

Core Knowledge

Teachers must deliver the knowledge and skills students need to meet these expectations to ensure students own the core knowledge, which is the foundation for higher-level thinking skills. Core knowledge involves the basics. Teachers determine what students know and need to know, therefore developing, nurturing, and expanding student skills. Whether a student reads a fiction or nonfiction book or article, uses mathematical operations to compute, solves multistep word problems, listens to rap or country music, or views Renaissance or abstract art, there is a basic core knowledge he or she recognizes, acknowledges, explores, and embraces.

Heidi Hayes Jacobs (2012) speaks of the *core* as "what is at the heart of teaching and learning" (pp. vii–viii). Harvey Silver, Thomas Dewing, and Matthew Perini (2012) provide teachers with core, research-based strategies, referring to literacy and thinking skills. Core knowledge includes solid literacy and mathematics skills and the ability to think critically across the grades and disciplines—from science to music, history, art, world languages, and more.

This book offers interventions, instructional coaching strategies, and curriculum lessons and resources to help learners gain core knowledge and excellent life outcomes. Without meaning attached to classroom practice and life applications, knowledge exists in a vacuum. Curriculum standards achieve meaning in instructional moments that offer multiple strategies delivered in multiple locations (Bridges-Rhoads & Van Cleave, 2016).

Ultimately, students must be the ones who hold the core knowledge in their hands, hearts, and brains. However, sometimes the texts that we use are "imbued with power" (Compton-Lilly, 2011, p. 432). The knowledge in a textbook is important, but it cannot be an entity unto itself. Teacher wisdom that goes beyond the textbook pages includes the knowledge of how to instruct a diverse student population.

Structure of This Book

Navigating the Core Curriculum: RTI Strategies to Support Every Learner offers strategies for general and special educators, student support teams, curriculum supervisors, instructional coaches, related service providers, and administrators. These strategies are connected to individual learner characteristics, classroom instructional practice, and core knowledge. University professors for preservice teachers, new teachers, and veteran teachers will also benefit from this resource since it offers practical ways to build mastery of core knowledge. The takeaways (or main ideas) offer research-based teaching and learning practices that help engage all students—high achieving, at grade level, below proficient, and those with behavioral issues—in diverse classrooms.

The goal of this book is to replace anxieties and apprehensions with RTI despite "travel obstacles" educators may encounter on the journey.

Each chapter of this book includes the following elements.

> **Evidence-based practice:** Evidence-based practice includes, but is not limited to, instructional designs with differentiated instruction and multiple *engagements* (activities or other methods to teach a concept) through a universal design for learning (UDL) approach—taking into account the why, what, and how of learning. Multiple engagements promote more than knowing the facts

but value how to increase interest, curiosity, and the overall motivation to learn. Teachers must offer instruction that is varied and responsive to learner diversity by mimicking the interactive and varied stimuli offered outside the classroom and allow students to "play" with core concepts rather than memorize facts.

> **Multiple curriculum entry points:** The sample lessons in this book show K–12 teachers how to teach concepts or learning goals in ways that engage students. Multiple curriculum entry points require viewing the curriculum through a lens that allows students of diverse levels entry to the core knowledge. This includes activities that invoke and value academic, behavioral, social, emotional, and cultural connections. The lessons cross all disciplines and grade levels.

Chapter 1 discusses how we can open the door for all learners by offering successful strategies and mindsets that bring together the RTI variables of classroom dynamics and teacher expertise into a cohesive framework with prescriptive, responsive, and contextually engaging tasks. This chapter provides tiered literacy and mathematics scenarios for RTI, along with successful strategies and mindsets. Implications for oral expression, listening comprehension, reading fluency and comprehension, vocabulary development, and mathematical computations and applications are offered.

Chapter 2 discusses how to approach the core vocabulary in reference to vocabulary development and early literacy skills. This chapter helps teachers determine student knowledge and select and implement the appropriate vocabulary interventions.

This process starts with identification that leads to interventions and, in turn, internalization of core knowledge and skills. This chapter provides the strategies, tools, and resources to achieve success in vocabulary, whether students are at grade level, require enrichment, or are in need of intervention. It provides elementary, middle school, and high school lessons to fuel vocabulary knowledge at different learner levels.

Chapter 3 acknowledges that students exist on a spectrum, with different levels of knowledge, interests, and motivation. These differences do not deter students from achieving multiple levels of success, since multitiered systems of supports appropriately acknowledge these differences with responsive, evidence-based interventions. This chapter explores screening and evaluation for behavior, literacy, and mathematics. It also demonstrates how instruction, practice, repetition, and application are valued, with an emphasis on how universal design for learning and differentiated instruction live and breathe in K–12 classrooms.

Chapter 4 discusses implementing best practices under the RTI umbrella and outlines how RTI addresses literacy and mathematical skills. It explores a multitiered system of supports with accommodations and modifications for strategic fluency with both academics and behavior in K–12 lessons. This chapter acknowledges that no one is born fluent in reading, writing, and mathematics skills and emphasizes the importance of tiered, cross-curricular connections and the support required to achieve successful learner outcomes. The chapter also emphasizes the importance of changing students' roles as passive recipients of knowledge to ones of active learners.

Chapter 5 explores learner variability with student-specific tiers that value quality instruction and a collaborative, problem-solving approach. Evidence-based practice includes structuring academics and behaviors with multitiered interventions. This chapter offers sample lessons that infuse consistency; guided practice; modeling; multiple means of visual, auditory, and kinesthetic/tactile (VAKT) approaches; and specific and timely feedback through whole-class, small-group, and individualized instruction. The chapter also asserts that challenges are transformed into solutions with step-by-step planning, quality instruction, and assessment.

Chapter 6 discusses rigorous learning for all students. Teachers must minimize and maximize, fine-tune, and individualize strategic engagements and include varied pacing with opportunities for both repetition and enrichment. The chapter also discusses how the core knowledge must be strategically planned to engage students in independent, cooperative, and collaborative assignments. Strategic engagements offer students opportunities to increase their skills with metacognition of their own levels and how to achieve more gains. That means they know their starting points and believe that they can achieve these planned destinations. Instructional practices outlined in the lessons include direct instruction, cooperative learning, and peer supports within whole-class, small-group, and individualized settings.

Chapter 7 discusses teacher fidelity and professional development in preparing for and sustaining evidence-based practice for instruction. RTI routes should be planned and traveled with caution, scrutiny, and optimism. This chapter emphasizes that sustainability at the school level involves pragmatic applications that include teacher preparation with buy-in, supports, collaborative practices, ongoing feedback, coaching, and fidelity to the process. Teacher fidelity to offer responsive learning experiences ensures that RTI is effective at each tier.

Finally, the epilogue summarizes the book's main points and suggests ways that educators can embrace RTI in their classrooms and schools.

Next, chapter 1 begins our journey into the RTI process, opening doors to allow *every* student to reach his or her intended destination—learning at high levels!

CHAPTER 1

OPENING DOORS FOR ALL LEARNERS

Doors allow entrance. Entrance in this case means access to knowledge, which in turn translates to greater lifelong opportunities for students. If the academic core knowledge is to reach all students, then teachers must honor diversity with prescriptive and cohesive instructional frameworks. Oral expression, listening comprehension, reading fluency, reading comprehension, written expression, vocabulary development, and mathematics computations and applications are all skills that open doors for future strides. Students enter these doors through primary, secondary, and tertiary entry points, known as tiers in the RTI process. The lessons in this chapter offer literacy, mathematics, and behavioral examples that allow teachers to embrace RTI so that doors are open to all students to achieve. Figure 1.1 (page 10) illustrates the structure of this chapter.

Teachers must honor diversity with prescriptive and cohesive instructional frameworks.

RTI Variables

A variable is considered an element or a factor that is subject to change. Variables are not always as clear cut and identifiable as the ones in a mathematical equation, such as solving for the variable of x in $5x = 20$. However, as with this linear equation, RTI involves knowing how to isolate variables to figure out the solution. When teachers collaboratively problem solve, they can identify and isolate RTI variables. RTI's academic and behavioral equations require looking at variables that include learner performance levels and the discrete steps of required tasks. Teachers analyze these variables to determine which academic and behavioral skills require introduction, reinforcement, reteaching, and maintenance. Administrators, teachers, students, and families are ultimately the human variables who continually collaborate to support interventions.

Two of the most important RTI variables include classroom dynamics and teacher expertise, which we explore in the following sections.

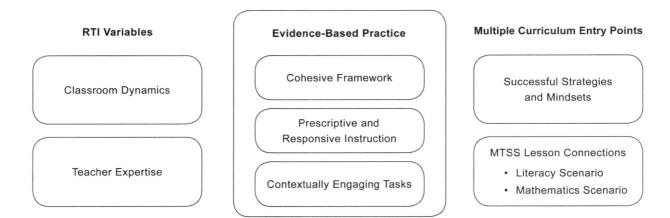

Figure 1.1: Plan for opening doors for all learners.

Administrators, teachers, students, and families are ultimately the human variables who continually collaborate to support interventions.

Classroom Dynamics

Planning student-specific, multitiered instruction is one way teachers positively influence classroom dynamics. Classroom dynamics include physical ones, such as the lighting, seating, and available resources, but emotional classroom dynamics are more important. These dynamics include setting up a classroom to value students as individuals within an accepting, trusting, and emotionally safe learning environment. Classroom dynamics value diverse interventions and multiple entry points for students at their instructional levels. Delivery should not frustrate students with learning that is too difficult or not within their prior knowledge base.

Just as navigation has several tools designed to increase movement, administrators should provide teachers with RTI supports, tools, and resources. This includes time to collaboratively plan, assess, tweak, and reflect on instruction.

Some students require additional instruction to hone skills with letter-sound correspondence, phoneme segmentation, fluency, word definitions, contextual clues, reading comprehension, mathematical practices, and behavior. Letters, words, sentences, numbers, shapes, motivation, attention, and good study skills are building blocks that allow students to understand, own, and apply concepts.

Teachers who realize that each student possesses different skill sets value not only the curriculum but also the student diversity present in every classroom. Depending on students' skill sets, teachers must adapt. Classroom dynamics affect the structured interactions between students and teachers.

Successful educators need to know their subjects. Subject knowledge goes beyond the content to knowing students as the most closely studied subjects. This includes knowing student backgrounds and interests. The first day of school is generally the first time we are introduced to our students, but the days that precede that encounter offer valuable instructional data. Each student brings his or her own backpack packed with strengths, weaknesses, and many prior home, school, and life experiences that shape him or her.

This includes exposure or lack of exposure to vocabulary through conversation, reading, and real-world and multimedia experiences.

Successful educators need to know their subjects.

Students do not come to us as clean slates. Most students come to us with positive and negative academic, social, emotional, and behavioral experiences. These events comprise the baseline core academic and behavioral levels *we must* identify. As students enter each grade from preschool to high school, we learn to recognize the many scripts that precede that first day of school.

When teachers communicate and students believe that they are malleable and able to learn the core knowledge, additional progress occurs, despite the challenges presented. Successful academic outcomes are influenced by resiliency and the belief that change is possible (Yeagar & Dweck, 2012). Positive mindsets influence academic achievements. Some students have uphill journeys to achieve the core knowledge, but that is when teachers collaboratively provide the appropriate scaffolding to help students succeed, despite their learning, behavioral, emotional, social, communicative, sensory, or physical differences. In modern classrooms, diversity is the norm. In turn, multiple engagements and personalized learning experiences with tiered instruction also must be the norm.

Everyone has a backstory, but students are more likely to achieve success when teachers plan for, prepare, and deliver solid instruction, positive attitudes, and multiple curriculum entry points. This includes motivating lesson plans that offer diverse, step-by-step interventions for the whole class, small groups, and individual students.

Lesson objectives must honor the academic core knowledge and also the class dynamics of the teacher's audience—a diverse cast of characters known as students.

Teacher Expertise

Programs do not teach, but teachers do. Teacher expertise begins at the early stage of preservice at the university level and continually expands in school settings. A teacher's development and expertise never stagnate. Universal screening and progress monitoring yield the appropriate selection of interventions for core instruction, but teachers need to make effective choices to honor an alternate way to identify students who need more intensive instruction or intervention (Wehman, 2013).

Programs do not teach, but teachers do.

After appropriate screening, teachers plan how abstract concepts are solidified in students' working memories. Teachers must introduce and then reinforce concepts. The strategies they use go beyond direct instruction to involve cooperative learning and developing collaborative partnerships with other teachers, intervention specialists, instructional leaders, families, and students.

However, before any instruction occurs, teachers must conduct accurate assessment. According to William Bender (2012), "Assessment tools in the differentiated class should be selected by the teacher to specifically target discrete skills on which a student is struggling" (p. 111). Teachers must be able to identify the skills with which students need more assistance, and then choose the appropriate, evidence-based materials to implement Tier 2 and 3 interventions.

Teachers should use RTI as a vehicle, with formative assessments in the front seat to guide instructional decisions and interventions. They offer students assistance in RTI tiers, but it is important to note that the interventions are not exclusively teacher owned; students must learn to own their strategies. Once teachers determine that interventions are effective, they can modify and adapt them based on the data from both formal and informal assessments. Some students may need increased interventions, while some may require decreased interventions as time goes on. If students continually master the core curriculum, then teachers should be cognizant of how interventions are helping, not enabling, students.

Evidence-Based Practice

RTI includes evidence-based practices, but there is no universal definition for RTI based on a one-size-fits-all approach, since one size basically fits none. Although teachers often use evidence-based literacy and mathematics resources as part of the interventions, RTI is not a neatly packaged program (Scanlon, 2013); the multitiered levels structure classroom instruction. The following sections describe the basic tenets of RTI: cohesive framework, prescriptive and responsive instruction, and contextually engaging tasks.

Cohesive Framework

The RTI framework is cohesive, multitiered, and research based. Cohesiveness includes organization and structure. Core instruction, student-specific interventions, screening instruments, progress monitoring, and data analysis are integral to RTI (Gersten & Vaughn, 2009). Progress monitoring includes estimating rates of student improvement and identifying adequate student progress.

When implemented with fidelity, RTI improves instructional quality to increase students' chance of school success as they move on to postsecondary choices in colleges and careers (McInerney & Elledge, 2013).

Teachers make data-based decisions regarding using supplementary intervention for students who do not respond to the core instruction delivered in Tier 1. The teacher delivers the core in whole-class, small-group, and individual instruction. Basically, educators deliver core instruction in the continuum of support shown in figure 1.2. This inverted pyramid demonstrates educators' collective responsibility for student learning by schoolwide teams and collaborative teacher teams. As noted, Tier 1 can also be referred to as primary instruction, Tier 2 as secondary instruction, and Tier 3 as tertiary instruction.

Prescriptive and Responsive Instruction

RTI is a prescriptive and responsive way to address student skill levels and needs. For many years, special education was the antithesis to the philosophy that one size fits all, some, or even most. But now, differentiated instruction supports all students in inclusive settings (Tomlinson, 1999). Ableism cannot replace individualization, nor should students be viewed from a deficit paradigm (Fierros, 2006). Prescriptive instruction acknowledges and responds to different abilities with tiered levels that occur in mixed-ability classrooms (Karten, 2015; Tomlinson, 1999). Fidelity to the programs teachers select is essential, but teachers also need to acknowledge that students do not fit into neatly wrapped packages. RTI is not a path to special educational services but a way to infuse good teaching practices that strengthen those areas in which students need improvement.

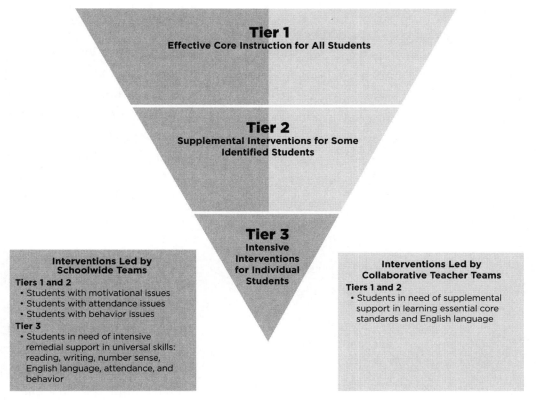

Source: *Buffum et al., 2012.*

Figure 1.2: Team responsibilities in the inverted RTI pyramid.

Buffum and colleagues (2012) write:

> In the RTI process, schools do not delay in providing help for struggling students until they fall far enough behind to qualify for special education, but instead provide targeted and systematic interventions to all students as soon as they demonstrate need. . . . Some schools mistakenly view RTI as merely a new way to qualify at-risk students for special education and focus on trying a few token general education interventions before referring struggling students for traditional special education testing and placement. (pp. 1–2)

Just as a doctor prescribes medicine in the right dosage with a policy of "do no harm," teachers must select interventions that consider benefits versus the risks with scrutiny and respect for learner autonomy (Knott & Harding, 2014).

Evidence-based RTI considers the amount and length of tiered interventions with quantity and quality as well as the teachers' and students' integrity. In this context, integrity includes fidelity to evidence-based strategies and interventions that honor learner diversity.

Tier 2 usually occurs over a period of about two months, while Tier 3 may have a longer and more intensive duration. For example, Tier 2 may occur over a period of ten weeks as opposed to twenty weeks for Tier 3 (Sanford, Harlacher, & Walker, 2010). These time frames are not standardized, since the length of tier instruction is responsive to learner progress. Appropriate student information in response to the multitiered interventions informs decisions and ultimately drives positive outcomes.

Contextually Engaging Tasks

Academic and behavioral tasks exist within the context of the core curriculum, but more important, within the context of real life. Student learning becomes more meaningful when students engage in context-related tasks with accompanying remediation and enrichment. RTI's evidence-based systematic interventions focus on student needs, but when these interventions are contextually based, teachers can establish relevancy for students. Real-world connections link concepts to learner interests to increase time on task and student buy-in with the motivation to learn more.

The following are examples of skills taught within contextually engaging tasks.

> **Oral expression:** Students cooperatively organize notes in small groups of three to five peers as they deliver a class presentation. Topics include a favorite family celebration, best day in school, or a difficult task accomplished.

> **Listening comprehension:** Students receive background information before viewing a clip from a popular movie or television show. They take notes with guided questions in a cloze structure in which they fill in key concepts to guide their listening.

> **Reading fluency:** Students read jokes and riddles with classmates before creating and presenting mathematics, science, and social studies jokes based on the vocabulary they are studying. The teacher shares a video with examples and nonexamples of fluency with expression, pausing, phrasing, and inflection with choral modeling, and offers instruction, feedback, and guidance to smaller groups and individual students.

> **Reading comprehension:** After students receive refreshers on specific types of reading comprehension questions (for example, main idea, sequencing, and so on), they form groups of three to four. Then each group selects a specific fairy tale, fable, or nonfiction article to analyze and writes comprehension questions to exchange with another cooperative group. Afterward, the groups discuss the reading comprehension skills gained with the teacher and the class.

> **Vocabulary development:** Students highlight a list of vocabulary words as they follow along on copies of lyrics from curriculum-related hip-hop videos from Flocabulary (www.flocabulary .com); for example, "The Week in Rap," "Geography," "Ancient History," and "Internet Safety."

> **Written expression:** Students write on topics that interest them (for example, fashion, NASCAR racing, soccer, dolphins, or beaded wrap bracelets). They use multiple scaffolding tools, such as transitional word lists, sensory words, online visual dictionaries, glossaries, writing frames, and technology tools.

> **Mathematical computations and applications:** Students complete engaging activities (for example, measuring ingredients for a recipe, figuring out the batting average of a baseball player, recording the average weekly and monthly temperatures) to learn reasoning.

Multiple Curriculum Entry Points

English philosopher Herbert Spencer (Brainy Quote, n.d.) wrote: "The great aim of education is not knowledge but action." Even though teachers arrange instructional activities to increase student knowledge, both the students and teachers are active learners. Teachers learn about their students as they note progress with multitiered interventions. In *The Student-Centered Classroom*, author Leo Jones (2007) writes:

> The teacher's role is more that of a facilitator than instructor; the students are active participants in the learning process. The teacher helps to guide the students, manage their activities, and direct their learning. Being a teacher means helping people to learn; and, in a student-centered class, the teacher is a member of the class as a participant in the learning process. (p. 2)

That's where multiple curriculum entry points come in.

Successful Strategies and Mindsets

Successful strategies and mindsets allow for scaffolding, guiding, compacting, and reinforcing the core curriculum to connect to individual learner skill sets. The main goal of RTI is for *all* students to achieve. Buffum and colleagues (2012) assert: "Response to intervention (RTI) is our best hope to provide every child with the additional time and support needed to learn at high levels" (p. xiii).

Each RTI tier exemplifies that strategic teaching honors student ownership and hones skills with phonemic awareness and fluency; comprehension of fiction, narrative, and expository text; mathematics computations and concepts; and real-life applications of literacy and mathematics. Teachers with mindsets that hold high expectations for all students never marginalize either the concepts or student potential.

Teachers with mindsets that hold high expectations for all students never marginalize either the concepts or student potential.

MTSS Lesson Connections

The following literacy and mathematics scenarios are examples of multitiered responsive interventions that embrace RTI's tiered instruction. The lessons offer a glimpse into the RTI process in action. They invite teachers to connect tiered interventions to their own grade levels, disciplines, and students, and to consider the collaborative staff roles and who is responsible for interventions for the whole class, small groups, and individual learners. As teachers plan literacy and mathematics units, they must honor student-centered instruction with an eye on increasing listening skills, fluency, reading comprehension, vocabulary, written expression, oral expression, and critical thinking skills.

Literacy Scenario

This scenario takes place in a fourth-grade language arts lesson. For Tier 1, students read Cynthia Lord's (2008) book *Rules*. The book depicts the themes of differences and accepting others through exploring the relationship between two siblings, the main characters. Catherine's brother, David, has autism. Students search the book for text-based evidence in response to written questions, explore character traits, and write a book report. During core instruction, students participate in read-alouds, guided practice, and buddy reads. The teacher offers students characterization graphic organizers where students can record their thoughts, along with writing frames to assist with the book reports.

The teacher offers students who easily grasp the concepts nonfiction articles on autism to review and summarize and present their findings to the class. They compare and contrast the knowledge from the nonfiction autism resources to how Lord presents David. Some students in core instruction write a literary review of the novel, others act out scenes from the novel, and some create storyboards with hand-drawn or digitally created visuals.

For Tier 2, a few students receive literacy instruction in small groups in addition to the core instruction. These students require daily assistance to better understand how to interpret the text to identify the characters' appearances, actions, and thoughts. Students elaborate on the rules, such as explaining why a boy takes off his shirt to swim, but not his shorts; why no toys are allowed in the fish tank; and why late does not mean you are not coming. The tiered instruction offers students increased chances to discuss the plot, answer inferential questions, and practice and apply new vocabulary.

Some students need additional assistance with written expression and receive more intensive, small-group instruction on how to write a cohesive book report with a beginning, middle, and end that cites text-based evidence. This occurs during Tier 3 instruction. A few students receive additional scaffolding by listening to a digital version of the book on Audible (www.audible.com) so they can hear the correct fluency and pronunciation modeled. This allows students the opportunity to access the text to answer the comprehension questions and write the book report. Students receive mini reading and writing lessons to sequence and understand the events. With guidance, they independently and collaboratively complete *Rules* activity sheets (www.cynthialord.com/pdf/rules_worksheets.pdf).

Mathematics Scenario

This scenario takes place in a tenth-grade geometry class. The teacher introduces geometric models of theorems and mathematics vocabulary, and students learn to solve a complex geometric theorem. However, all students in the class do not grasp the concepts at identical speeds.

During Tier 1 instruction, students receive step-by-step procedures, engage in mathematics journaling, participate in think-alouds, and have access to manipulatives. In Tier 2, some students require small-group instruction, practice circle theorem applications, and receive instruction to strengthen weaker computational skills. These students have extended opportunities to practice the geometry skills with daily progress monitoring.

In Tier 3, a few students need more assistance to identify shapes within other shapes, since they are missing essential prior knowledge with many skill gaps about chords, diameters, arcs, and congruency. Another small group of students requires enrichment activities instead of repetition. The teacher prepares materials for learning centers and invites students to cooperatively explore them. Pattern blocks, pegboards, compasses, rulers, solid 3-D shapes, and virtual manipulatives are available for additional student exploration, reinforcement, and enrichment. The teacher offers instruction in tiers, giving students time to practice, refine, and own the skills and concepts.

Conclusion

Teachers must continually synthesize and tweak the instructional routes they choose based on the data—student progress. Chapter 1 began this journey. Literacy and mathematics navigation requires inviting classroom dynamics where all students can learn in an accessible, nonthreatening environment as well as teacher expertise in delivering a multitiered system of supports. G. Rexlin Jose (2015) frames the learning conversation and guides the way as we continue to navigate the core curriculum: "Vocabulary is the gateway to knowledge that unlocks the doors of sublime ideas to the readers" (p. 7).

Chapter 2 follows with an exploration of the academic language—the core vocabulary.

APPROACHING THE CORE VOCABULARY

Literacy involves applying reading, writing, language, and critical-thinking skills. Vocabulary, a building block of literacy, describes events, plots, people, and places. Vocabulary explains actions, expands thoughts, and increases conceptual understanding (Sprenger, 2013). Some students have more exposure to vocabulary at home than others, so the instruction at school must attend to that diversity in exposure.

> *Vocabulary instruction includes more than memorizing definitions.*

Vocabulary instruction includes more than memorizing definitions. Providing graphical representations of words, transforming unknown vocabulary into a student's own words, mapping, reading selections aloud, performing skits, and playing cooperative word games all exemplify ways to connect vocabulary to students. The evidence-based practices in this chapter help teachers assist their students to explore and embrace vocabulary as they read, speak, write, think, and interact with text and people.

Figure 2.1 (page 20) illustrates the structure of this chapter.

Academic Language

Vocabulary is an indispensable part of language, whether a student is a first or second language learner (Wangru, 2016). Students with different reading levels and vocabulary exposure have different starting points when they enter schools, in terms of their exposure to vocabulary. Some learners have home environments with families who read to them, and other students have fewer words spoken and limited literacy experiences. Research shows that developing vocabulary skills facilitates richer listening, speaking, and writing abilities (Jose, 2015). However, ways to effectively incorporate vocabulary instruction within a given class period often challenges teachers (Robb, Sinatra, & Eschenauer, 2014). Vocabulary

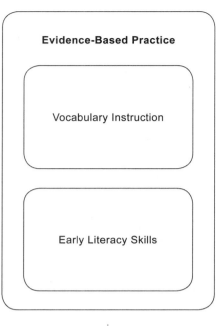

Academic Language

Identify Vocabulary for Students With and Without IEPs

Determine Student Levels

Select Appropriate Interventions

Evidence-Based Practice

Vocabulary Instruction

Early Literacy Skills

Multiple Curriculum Entry Points

How to Identify Knowledge, Intervene, and Ensure Internalization

MTSS Lesson Connections
- Grade 3 Lesson on Viking Culture
- Grade 8 Vocabulary Lesson on the Federalists
- Grade 10 Vocabulary Lesson on Global Warming
- PRO-Vocabulary Instruction

Figure 2.1: Plan for approaching the core vocabulary.

navigation is therefore complex, but as this chapter shows, it is also very navigable when a teacher utilizes RTI and systematic strategies.

Identify Vocabulary for Students With and Without IEPs

Like RTI, vocabulary is divided into three tiers (Beck, McKeown, & Kucan, 2002); however, these are not related to tiers of intervention but instead, to content. Tier1 includes frequently used words, or basic vocabulary words that generally have one meaning. Tier 2 words are found across content areas with multiple meanings, and Tier 3 words are subject specific. Respectively, words such as *book*, *happy*, *love*, or *friend* would be considered Tier 1 words, while *compare*, *justify*, *draft*, and *exemplify* would be categorized as Tier 2 words. Finally, Tier 3 words would be discipline related, such as *constitution*, *meiosis*, *circumference*, and *witticism*.

Students require mastery of academic language to achieve literacy success (Soto & Calderón, 2016). This means teachers must select strategies that teach

appropriate high-frequency and discipline-specific words across the curriculum, whether that text is informational or fiction. Vocabulary instruction is not incidental but must include explicit strategies that allow students to own the academic language in print and non-print conversations and interactions.

> *Vocabulary instruction is not incidental but must include explicit strategies.*

Acquiring academic language is often difficult for students with and without identified differences, including those with IDEA disability and cultural diversity. Physically demonstrating a word or a visual can assist an English learner (EL) to better understand a word that may not even exist in his or her own language or have a multiple meaning (Colorín Colorado, 2015). Students with and without individualized education programs (IEPs), ELs, and those with varying language, literacy experiences, and acumens need to construct meanings for written and spoken words.

This knowledge is within all students' reach when instruction faithfully uses evidence-based practices with multitiered instruction. RTI is a complex process involving (1) determining student levels and (2) selecting appropriate interventions.

Determine Student Levels

Responsive vocabulary interventions include whole-class, small-group, and individual instruction. Teachers can determine a student's vocabulary knowledge through informal and formal written and oral measurements, inventories, and assessments of words in isolation and in context. They collect data on student progress with identification and word meaning to guide and adapt instruction. Vocabulary tests may follow various formats—standardized, teacher created, or online. The following websites offer examples of vocabulary tests and exercises that focus on definitions, parts of speech, synonyms, antonyms, and vocabulary usage in sentences.

- ➢ VocabTest.com (www.vocabtest.com)
- ➢ VocabularySize.com (http://my .vocabularysize.com)
- ➢ Merriam-Webster's Learner's Dictionary (http://learnersdictionary.com/quiz /vocabulary-start)

Select Appropriate Interventions

Varying the engagements, representations, actions, and expressions honors learner diversity. For example, varying representations means that the information is not just displayed one way, whether that is auditory or visual. Multiple media representations expand students' transfer and application of language and concepts. Teachers should use specific tools and strategies to build fluencies and motivation to honor students' varying prior knowledge and inspire interest. The following research-based interventions

connect to individual students and multitiered groupings (Jose, 2015; Maiullo, 2016; Rimbey, McKeown, Beck, & Sanora, 2016; Robb et al., 2014; Wangru, 2016). Teachers can:

- ➢ Provide informal and frequent understanding checks
- ➢ Implement daily, weekly, and monthly reviews of prior learning
- ➢ Offer students ways to figure out unfamiliar vocabulary with each step explained, such as:
  - • Read the word in the context of a sentence.
  - • Read the sentence with a blank used in place of the word.
  - • Substitute a word that makes sense.
  - • Look up the word with an online tool (such as WordHippo [http:// www.wordhippo.com]), a handheld dictionary, or a text's glossary.
- ➢ Appropriately scaffold literacy instruction
- ➢ Value diverse representations
- ➢ Pace the delivery of content
- ➢ Provide modeling
- ➢ Offer direct, guided instruction and then independent practice
- ➢ Show examples and nonexamples
- ➢ Practice think-alouds
- ➢ Ask students to explain their work
- ➢ Personalize vocabulary with individualized student lists and pictures of words next to their definitions (Pics4Learning [www.pics4learning.com])
- ➢ Instruct on phonemic awareness and structural analysis
- ➢ Monitor reader response journals

➤ Provide compartmentalization (for example, character perspective charts)

➤ Reinforce self-questioning

➤ Offer detailed and timely feedback

➤ Reteach and enrich as necessary

Evidence-Based Practice

The National Reading Technical Assistance Center compiles research on vocabulary acquisition and instruction (Butler et al., 2010). Research synthesis highlights the merits of direct instruction and learning beyond definitional knowledge, which means learning a word's definition as well as what it means in context. Students need to have a command of vocabulary when they speak, read, hear, and write. This involves receptive language in which students are interpreting words, and using or producing language in conversation as well as in print (Kamil & Hiebert, 2005). This understanding includes, but is not limited to, hearing abundant vocabulary that may or may not be within a student's prior knowledge or interests.

Students also need to know how to interpret vocabulary on standardized testing. Active learning, personalization of word learning, increased word knowledge, and repeated exposure to the words help learners understand vocabulary (Blachowicz & Fisher, 2000). Implementing effective vocabulary instruction and supporting early literacy skills allow students to understand the core vocabulary (Rimbey et al., 2016).

Vocabulary Instruction

Academic and behavioral growth within the general education classroom requires students to access and master core vocabulary. Skills such as identifying academic vocabulary, citing text-based evidence from literature and informational text, creating dynamic essays, evaluating algebraic expressions, and solving multistep word problems all require good teaching practices that connect the reading, writing, mathematical, and cross-curricular vocabulary to students in motivating ways. Applying the vocabulary to build conceptual knowledge is imperative because of curriculum demands and reading complexities as students advance through the grades.

Academic vocabulary enhances students' understanding of the disciplines. A broader term—*academic literacy*—is dependent on the contexts within which students practice the literacy (Baumann & Graves, 2010). In school settings, academic literacy connects to the reading proficiency required in content-specific texts and literature (Torgesen et al., 2007). Therefore, effective vocabulary instruction should offer repeated exposure to words, definitional and contextual information, and active, meaningful engagement.

Early Literacy Skills

Teachers must assess students' early literacy skills through phonological and print awareness with guided questions, oral reads, and word identification to ensure that the next step of appropriate instruction follows. Screening and progress monitoring at set times during the year then steer the tiered instruction. Phonics inventories include teachers synthesizing and analyzing how students pronounce academic vocabulary, which then shed light on students' basic phonemic skills.

These inventories assess skill levels with phonemic awareness, fluency, and the comprehension of fiction, narrative, and expository text. Informal reading inventories analyze skills such as oral reading, comprehension, and word identification. This may include activities such as reading graded word lists, real and pseudo words, and passages. Teachers assess students on their responses to oral questions and vocabulary comprehension within passages and sentences and from word lists. Every content area and concept has its own vocabulary that teachers must identify and analyze for students with diverse reading skills and levels.

Every content area and concept has its own vocabulary that teachers must identify and analyze for students with diverse reading skills and levels.

It is vital that families provide a literacy-rich environment at home to reinforce skills and objectives with their children. Families can encourage their children to identify, pronounce, decode, and encode letters and sounds in isolation and within words in road signs, recipes, grocery stores, and newspapers. For example, while cooking spaghetti, parents can have their child identify final sounds of words, practice phoneme segmentation, and read the box directions.

Daily and functional reads of fiction and nonfiction genres partner schools and homes, with students gaining many transferrable literacy skills. Functional reads include students' everyday interactions with words displayed in books, video games, websites, newspapers, and more. The idea is for the reading to have function and meaning for each student, with school reads being fun ones too, not just viewed as assignments. Families can encourage good reading practices by modeling reading for their children, whether it is a newspaper, paperback book, or electronic device. Families can also read together, with schools offering book lists and strategies to promote increased literacy.

The reproducible "Phonemic Awareness and Fluency Record" (page 35) is a tool to help students begin, advance, and fine-tune phonemic awareness skills, while the reproducible "Comprehension of Fiction, Narrative, and Expository Text" (page 36) helps teachers evaluate students' skills in comprehending fiction, narrative, and expository text. These tools increase teacher knowledge of student levels as they plan their lessons.

Teachers can collect this information to help develop student phonemic awareness, fluency, and reading comprehension profiles to identify learners' baseline levels. They then use this knowledge to select interventions that address the specific areas that challenge students as they read more difficult vocabulary. Teachers can always advance and fine-tune students' literacy skills, but identification is the initial step that begins the process.

Teachers can always advance and fine-tune students' literacy skills, but identification is the initial step that begins the process.

Multiple Curriculum Entry Points

The following curriculum examples help teachers identify students' vocabulary needs and then engage students in productive application of the words across disciplines, without allowing complex vocabulary to interfere with conceptual understanding. A student may not understand a word because he or she does not know how to pronounce it. The teacher might then offer strategies to help that student decode a multisyllabic word, identify syllable types, pronounce consonant digraphs, or determine structural analysis. Students might know how to decode a word but cannot categorize or apply meaning in context. Teachers can portray words in deeper ways that allow for increased internalization. Establishing the proficiency levels determines the remediation required. Three steps—(1) identify knowledge, (2) intervene, and (3) ensure internalization—ultimately lead to strategies that allow students to prioritize, relate, and own the vocabulary.

How to Identify Knowledge, Intervene, and Ensure Internalization

With RTI, the teacher identifies students' vocabulary knowledge, intervenes with strategies, and ensures that students internalize the core vocabulary. He or she can accomplish this through whole-class instruction in Tier 1, smaller targeted groups in Tier 2, and more intensive instruction in Tier 3.

Identify Knowledge

Teachers can use the chart in figure 2.2 to note word-identification levels with a step-by-step approach, showing proficiency as well as need for remediation. Teachers listen to students read individually, in small groups, and during whole-class instruction. However, teachers should never ask a student to read aloud if he or she will be embarrassed. Due to time parameters, another option is to allow students to read into digital devices that staff, such as general and special education teachers, reading interventionists, speech-language

pathologists, paraprofessionals, and the students themselves can review to note proficiencies. Hearing specific examples helps students develop metacognition.

> *Hearing specific examples helps students develop metacognition.*

Teachers jot down words or sentences that raise concerns. For example, if a student reads the word *wildlife* as *filewild* that would indicate that he or she is transposing words; or if a student reads *grandma's seventieth birthday* as *grandma's seventeenth birthday*, this word error most certainly affects comprehension. The chart does not include every word-identification skill, but it encourages teachers to think about what errors mean in terms of their next instructional steps.

Intervene

Teachers intervene and monitor with strategies that provide systematic and explicit vocabulary instruction. They share fiction and nonfiction books with oral reads, along with guided and independent practice across genres, disciplines, and multimedia formats, including vocabulary pictures and examples of word relationships. Students highlight words in text to increase recognition and appropriately demonstrate their

Word Identification, Concepts, and Vocabulary Skills	Proficient (above 80 percent)	Needs Remediation (below 80 percent)
Vowel and consonant sounds (initial, medial, beginning)		
Consonant digraphs		
Word meaning		
Syllables		
Compound words		
Word categories		

Figure 2.2: Word identification, concepts, and vocabulary skills exercise.

ownership of the vocabulary across disciplines. Teachers activate the text-to-speech feature for online sites to increase fluency with models and offer feedback, guidance, and instruction.

Ensure Internalization

Finally, teachers must ensure students achieve and own vocabulary competency with transfer and application to other reading materials. Students establish personalized vocabulary connections through writing, conversation, and diverse engagements. When students internalize the vocabulary, they own it. This occurs through interactive vocabulary practice with words that include, but are not limited to, reflecting on prior knowledge from KWL (what I know, what I want to know, what I learned) charts, word mapping, and other graphic organizers, and practicing word usage with peers, songs, games, and skits.

The National Council of Teachers of English (NCTE) offers concrete, visual ways for students to internalize vocabulary with word mapping and more on their ReadWriteThink website (www.readwritethink.org). Playing games such as Balderdash to determine correct word meanings, solving crossword puzzles, or pantomiming words are also viable ways to ensure vocabulary internalization beyond a skill-and-drill approach.

MTSS Lesson Connections

The following elementary, middle, and high school lessons apply the identify knowledge, intervene, and ensure internalization approach across multiple content areas. (Visit **go.SolutionTree .com/RTI** to access more free reproducible lesson examples.)

Grade 3 Lesson on Viking Culture

A third-grade social studies class is studying Viking culture. The topic may not be in students' prior knowledge, so when a learner completes a KWL chart, it helps teachers find out what students know or think they know.

Identify Knowledge

The teacher asks students to list everything they know about the Vikings, want to know, and learned at the end of the unit in the KWL chart. See figure 2.3 (page 26). For example, students responding that the Vikings football team from Minnesota chose its name to emulate the fierceness of a group that lived centuries ago might lead to a motivating discussion on Viking history.

Then, students use the tasks and guided questions in figure 2.4 (page 26) to practice the vocabulary they acquire during the lesson. The teacher identifies learner decoding and word application skills and levels. Just as the Vikings explored new lands, students need to explore and conquer these academic words to then understand the social studies content.

Intervene

The teacher might decide to subdivide the tasks or guided questions with additional scaffolding, so he or she can provide lists of word blends and have students practice the words in text. Teachers can use the graphic organizers in figure 2.5 (page 26) and figure 2.6 (page 27) as models to assist students with differing reading abilities and executive functioning skills to categorize words and syllables.

The teacher gives students fiction and nonfiction passages, ranging from those in a social studies text to online reads, such as ReadWorks' (2015) "Long Live the Vikings" (www.readworks.org/passages /long-live-vikings) to fictional stories and fables about Viking gods with multimedia presentations, such as those at BrainPOP Educators' (n.d.) "Lesson Ideas: Vikings" (https://educators.brainpop .com/bp-topic/vikings). He or she presents the concepts in sequential and manageable steps, from simple to complex, to minimize confusion.

Viking KWL		
K (what I know about the Vikings)	**W (what I want to know about the Vikings)**	**L (what I learned about the Vikings)**
The Vikings are a football team.	What happened to the Vikings?	The football team chose its name because they are fierce, like the Vikings were. The Vikings were seafarers who raided villages and settled many lands in the Scandinavian region.
I know that they were explorers who lived a long time ago.	What does the word *Viking* mean? When did they live?	*Viking* means piracy. The Vikings lived from about 787–1086 CE.
The Vikings invaded a lot of places.	How did they lose power?	The Vikings lost control as the population in Scandinavia changed and Christianity spread. There are theories about their decline, but no one knows for sure.

Figure 2.3: KWL chart for Vikings lesson.

Word Identification, Concepts, and Vocabulary Skills	Tasks and Guided Questions
Consonant sounds	What is the beginning sound in the word *Vikings*?
Consonant digraphs	Name a consonant digraph in the word *shipbuilding*.
Word meaning	Offer a synonym for the word *saga*.
Syllables	Identify the number and types of syllables in these words: *navigation, warrior, battle, Atlantic Ocean*.
Compound words	Break up these compound words into their parts: *shipbuilding, longboats, seafarers*.
Word categories	Place these words under the headings of *people, places*, or *things*: *skuta, fiord, Leif Erikson, Scandinavia, cauldron, Atlantic Ocean, Vikings, shipbuilding, warrior, oarsman, Norway, gold, invaders, continent, invasion*.

Figure 2.4: Tasks and guided questions for Vikings lesson.

People	Places	Things
Leif Erikson	Atlantic Ocean	cauldron
Vikings	Scandinavia	shipbuilding
warrior	fiord	skuta
oarsman	Norway	gold
invaders	continent	invasion

Figure 2.5: Categorization chart for Vikings lesson.

Ensure Internalization

Finally, the teacher allows students to practice their new vocabulary in various ways to ensure they internalize the learning, including performing arts with Viking collages, skits, interpretive dances, and songs. Some students write captions for Viking clipart (Classroom Clipart [http://bit.ly/2eiELKH]).

To help students internalize their learning, teachers invite them to participate in a think-pair-share activity. Think-pair-share is a cooperative way to engage learners in small-group structured discussions to help them understand the content (Rubinstein-Avila, 2013). Teachers give students

Syllable Types					
Closed	**Vowel-Consonant-e**	**Open Syllables**	**Vowel Teams**	**_r_-Controlled**	**Consonant-_le_**
<u>ship</u>	<u>grave</u>	<u>re</u>-gion (first syllable is open)	<u>raids</u>	<u>ar</u>-ti-facts (first syllable is _r_-controlled)	bat-<u>tle</u> (second syllable)
At-lan-tic (all three syllables are closed)	in-vade (second syllable)	Vi-kings (first syllable is open)	Leif	Norse	peo-ple (second syllable)
Vi-kings (second syllable is closed)		pi-ra-cy	soil	plun-der (second syllable)	
			spear	sword	

Figure 2.6: Syllables chart for Vikings lesson.

time to independently engage with the text and then connect or pair with another student or group to expand their knowledge. Linguistic engagements accompany the textual ones. Think-pair-share is effective for increasing intrinsic motivation and also has implications for students with different language proficiencies (Shih & Reynolds, 2015). In this case, students read brief passages and have small-group discussions about what they read and learned—the Viking takeaways. Of course, this example includes invited application across multiple subjects and grades.

Grade 8 Vocabulary Lesson on the Federalists

I once observed an eighth-grade social studies teacher lecture her students on the Federalist period in U.S. history. Slowly, she began to lose the students' attention. They somewhat listened as the teacher and other students read the history text. The teacher periodically stopped the reading to ask low-level comprehension questions.

Later, I had a coaching session with the teacher and asked if she ever thought about engaging students in an activity to better help them understand the Federalist period and its relevant vocabulary words. She responded that she used to do a Federalist tug-of-war activity, show videos, and assign group research projects, but there was no time for that anymore. Ouch! I shared that students would not remember the words or concepts in a unit unless they are actively involved with multiple experiences. I encourage teachers to try the following steps to help students learn the Federalist concepts and vocabulary.

> *Think-pair-share is a cooperative way to engage learners in small-group structured discussions to help them understand the content.*

Identify Knowledge

Figure 2.7 (page 28) offers various ways a teacher can engage students with historical words and events through word exploration and critical-thinking activities.

Word Identification, Concepts, and Vocabulary Skills	Tasks and Guided Questions
Affixes and roots	Tell how the prefix *anti-* changes the word *Federalist*.
Document-based vocabulary reference materials	Define these words in the context of the Ninth and Tenth Amendments: *enumeration, construed, disparage, retained, delegated, reserved, prohibited, respectively*.
Picture prompt	Write a paragraph about the people and actions in the historical pictures seen at the TeachingAmericanHistory.org website (Lloyd, 2016; http://teachingamericanhistory.org/convention/stearns).
Syllables	Identify the numbers and types of syllables in these words: *Constitution, confederation, Federalists, ratification, compromise*.
Classification	Sort words into nouns, verbs, adjectives, and adverbs.
Compare and contrast	Explore Hamilton and Jefferson's opposing views at the Public Broadcasting Service (PBS, 2007) site, "Alexander Hamilton: People & Events—Creating the U.S. Constitution" (http://to.pbs.org/2f5U4T9). Record answers in a Venn diagram. Hamilton vs. Jefferson

Figure 2.7: Federalist word tasks and guided questions.

Intervene

Teachers ask students to reword and divide more difficult questions into their components for students. For example, instead of asking students to delineate why Hamilton objected to the constitutional proposals for civilian rule and military strength, the teacher could say, "Explain who Hamilton was and why he did not want civilian rule. Offer examples of constitutional proposals at this time and how Hamilton felt about the U.S. government's military strength."

Ensure Internalization

Finally, teachers can have students participate in a kinesthetic debate to explore the concepts and share viewpoints to ensure they internalize the learning. Students stand by corresponding numbers on a number line that is posted on the floor to express their agreements and disagreements. The teacher uses sticky notes or sentence strips with the negative and positive numbers listed. As students share text-based statements, they listen to their peers and move to a different location on the number line if the fact-based opinions they hear sway them. This movement generates a vocabulary-rich class discussion and debate. The teacher instructs students to reference text-based vocabulary posted on a Federalist word wall.

Figure 2.8 shows how to set up the number line in the classroom. Algebra teachers will appreciate

−5	−4	−3	−2	−1	0	1	2	3	4	5
Strongly Disagree					Neutral					Strongly Agree

Figure 2.8: Federalist kinesthetic number line.

the mathematics reinforcement of negative and positive numbers in the social studies classroom. Teachers verbally and visually present statements to the class to assist students with different levels of listening and reading skills. He or she posts one descriptor at a time on an interactive board or PowerPoint slide. Students then move to the number that indicates their level of agreement or disagreement. The teacher can use the following debate prompts.

➢ Alexander Hamilton was correct to say that the Federal government should take over the unpaid debts of the states during the American Revolution.

➢ Thomas Jefferson was right to believe in the power of individual people, such as farmers, in favor of a strong central government.

➢ Federalists strengthened our government at the people's expense.

➢ Antifederalists were correct in thinking that more power should be placed with state and local governments.

During the debate, the teacher displays a word wall with an A–Z vocabulary list and asks students to select words and write a paragraph that demonstrates understanding (see figure 2.9). The A–Z listing offers students a way to plan and collect their thoughts. Students can also branch out with words other than nouns and add prefixes and affixes. After completing the list (there does not have to be a word next to every letter), students can use their words to generate a paragraph about the Federalists. The reproducible "A–Z Vocabulary List" (page 37) provides a blank template of a vocabulary list teachers can adapt to any lesson.

Federalist A–Z Vocabulary List	
A	Antifederalists
B	
C	centralized, Constitution. compromise, control
D	debt
E	economic, expense
F	Federalists, farmers, federal
G	government
H	Hamilton
I	individuals
J	Jefferson
K	
L	local
M	
N	national
O	objections
P	political, power
Q	
R	ratification
S	state, strength
T	taxes
U	unpaid
V	
W	weakness
X	
Y	
Z	
Select five words to use in a paragraph about Federalists.	My Federalist paragraph: In the eighteenth century, the U.S. *government* was forming. Thomas *Jefferson* and Alexander *Hamilton* had different ideas about who should have more *power*. *Jefferson* favored *local control*, while *Hamilton* wanted a strong central *government*. Thomas *Jefferson* believed that *power* belonged to *local*, *state*, and *individual* people, such as *farmers*, instead of having a strong central government. Alexander *Hamilton* felt the opposite way and wanted the *federal government* to be more powerful and make *economic* decisions. They finally reached a *compromise*.

Figure 2.9: Federalist word wall example.

Grade 10 Vocabulary Lesson on Global Warming

Sometimes lessons require warm-ups, including this one on global warming. Structural analysis and word identification require specific, discrete steps. Teachers can strengthen vocabulary identification with structural analysis and academically engaging activities. In this lesson on global warming, the teacher includes guided questions, multimedia presentations, and technology tools.

Identify Knowledge

Students may have an interest in global warming but be turned off during instruction due to the complexity of the words. In this lesson, the teacher instructs students how to break up the multisyllabic words into their parts with structural analysis, syllabication rules, lessons about consonant blends, and so on. Students complete the tasks and answer guided questions so the teacher can identify student strengths and weaknesses, as shown in figure 2.10.

The teacher also gives students National Geographic's (2016) global warming quiz (http://on.natgeo.com/1hfGRSW) to help assess their prior knowledge.

> *Teachers can strengthen vocabulary identification with structural analysis and academically engaging activities.*

Intervene

The teacher offers the following interventions to enliven the vocabulary with visuals, music, and study skill tools. These interventions engage students, pushing them to learn more. Some online and print articles and multimedia presentations the teacher offers include the following.

➢ Students read the online article, "What Is Global Warming?" (National Geographic, n.d.; http://on.natgeo.com/2dxH7CG) to provide additional information with digital formats, with the text-to-speech feature activated. The teacher asks students to highlight key vocabulary using digital tools or prints out the article for students to manually highlight the terms.

➢ The teacher shows clips from Al Gore's (Guggenheim, 2006) video

Word Identification, Concepts, and Vocabulary Skills	Tasks and Guided Questions
Structural analysis	Identify the base words of *global, environmental, recycling, biodiesel, dioxide, atmosphere*.
Consonant blends	Name a consonant blend in these words: *global, fluorescent, planet, bulb*.
Word meaning	Offer synonyms for *poisonous* and *environment*. Use online or handheld dictionaries and thesauruses.
Syllables	Identify the number and types of syllables in these words: *emissions, temperature, malaria, astronomer*.
Compound words	Break up these compound words into their parts: *greenhouse, rainfall, buildup*.
Word categories	Place these terms and concepts under the headings of *natural forces* or *human activity* in reference to global warming: *depleted fish population, extra carbon dioxide, glaciers disappearing, dense population, runaway greenhouse effects*.

Figure 2.10: Global warming words and questions.

An Inconvenient Truth (www.pbs.org /now/shows/304) while referencing key vocabulary.

Ensure Internalization

WebQuests, such as Zunal (http://zunal.com), increase inquiry via online research and access to a multitude of content. The structured framework, such as the one on global warming, has a step-by-step format that includes an introduction to the task, the process, an evaluation, and a conclusion. Students access resources and respond to content inquiry. Teachers can review and use WebQuests on an array of subjects across grades K–12 that are already posted on Zunal or create their own.

Students do the following in pairs or groups to investigate the effects of global warming.

> ➤ Read the WebQuest "Causes and Effects of Global Warming" (http://zunal.com/process.php?w=4527) to discover how natural and manmade air pollution, deforestation, and the earth's natural warming and cooling trends contribute to global warming.

> ➤ Respond to each other's cause-and-effect global warming questions.

After the step-by-step approach to identify knowledge, intervene, and ensure internalization, the vocabulary learning continues. Judy Willis (2006) reminds us that the more ways students can learn, the greater the relevancy to previously stored memories to create associations, discover patterns, and sort information. The next section on PRO-vocabulary instruction offers ways for students to prioritize, relate to, and own the vocabulary in elementary, middle school, and high school classrooms.

PRO-Vocabulary Instruction

The PRO strategy helps develop students' vocabulary proficiency. As part of PRO-vocabulary instruction, students:

> ➤ Prioritize the essential core words

> ➤ Relate the words to text and concepts

> ➤ Own the words by transferring the meaning to personal connections and ongoing application

RTI offers students the interventions, but sometimes it is an overwhelming task for vocabulary instruction, since students' background knowledge and real-world experiences with language differ. PRO-vocabulary instruction extracts the key vocabulary to create word associations and offer a framework that responds to vocabulary demands and learner differences.

The sample lessons in figures 2.11–2.13 (pages 32–33) connect basic (or core) vocabulary skills to elementary, middle school, and high school grade levels. These examples apply PRO-vocabulary instruction in three ways: to (1) an elementary reading lesson on Bill Brittain's (1983) novel *The Wish Giver: Three Tales of Coven Tree*, (2) a middle school science lesson on how living things interact in the biosphere, and (3) a high school lesson on trigonometry.

Literacy requires vocabulary instruction beyond memorization. Students soon forget vocabulary lists and memorized facts if learning has little emotional value or context to their lives (Willis, 2006). Isolated words must relate to the content so students have more reasons to own them. Varied experiences yield increased retention and application. Some students need help to pronounce the words, and some students need to know how to relate the words to written and oral contexts.

Elementary Lesson	The Wish Giver by Bill Brittain (1983)
Prioritize	Students define and pantomime words from the novel to explore essential vocabulary. Students categorize words into the headings of *nouns*, *verbs*, *adjectives*, and *adverbs* (for example, *wishes*, *granted*, *croaking*, *Jug-a-Rum*, *mortals*, *incredible*, *fraud*, *reluctance*, *dignified*, *flooded*).
Relate	Students relate the vocabulary to the story. For example, "The *wishes* were *granted*, but Thaddeus Blinn was an *incredible fraud*."
Own	Students use the words in personal sentences. For example, "I felt *incredible reluctance* when asked to do the work, but when I completed the assignment my *wish* to relax was *granted*."

The following occurs at each tier.

Tier 1: The teacher provides the whole class with direct skill instruction on the parts of speech. Students read the chapters in cooperative literature groups, and are assigned roles as passage picker, artful artist, connector, discussion director, and word wizard. Students then share responses to teacher-guided questions in small groups and whole-class instruction. The teacher monitors all groups' progress. Visit the NCTE website (www.readwritethink.org/classroom-resources/lesson-plans /literature-circles-getting-started-19.htm) for literature circle ideas.

Tier 2: A reading interventionist provides students at lower fluency and comprehension levels with explicit reading instruction. They analyze the story's structure and take timed sentence reading assessments. Sessions occur three times each week for forty-five-minute periods for eight to ten weeks.

Tier 3: One student in the class has a tested reading level three grade levels below the class. The school reading interventionist gives sixty-minute individualized reading remediation five days a week and monitors the student's progress.

Figure 2.11: Elementary reading PRO-vocabulary example.

Fluency, word application across texts, reading comprehension, and written expression are all skills that require discrete task analysis, which means offering a step-by-step approach that determines what specific vocabulary assistance students require. Identification then determines the level of intervention. Fluency and automaticity are reading partners in this journey. Students cannot be expected to cite evidence from literature and informational text, write dynamic essays, or solve multistep mathematical word problems if they do not have an adequate vocabulary to draw from.

Learning is not regurgitating facts but the retention of meaningful experiences that the student owns. Memorizing definitions may allow a student to score well on a matching or multiple-choice test, but it will not create critical thinkers. Beyond memorization means that the learning remains memorable

with ways to prioritize, internalize, relate, and own the vocabulary and concepts. Deeper understandings occur when learners use the vocabulary in a variety of imaginative ways that include increased dialogue, peer teaching, vocabulary theater skits, and cooperative groups (Robb et al., 2014).

> *Isolated words must relate to the content so students have more reasons to own them.*

The reproducible "PRO-Vocabulary Instruction" (page 38) provides an effective tool that students can use to expand vocabulary proficiencies and prioritize core words, relate them to the text, and *own* the words as they read, speak, write, and think across subjects.

Middle School Lesson	How Living Things Interact in the Biosphere
Prioritize	The teacher introduces these vocabulary words and terms to the class: *biosphere, lithosphere, atmosphere, hydrosphere, population, interdependent, organisms, ecosystem, interact, community, consumers, producers, human activity, food chain, individual, niche, compose, decompose, extinct, predator, prey.*
Relate	The teacher helps students relate the words to one another. He or she generates a study of affixes and root words with direct instruction on how the root word sphere is transformed with the prefixes *litho*, which refers to stone; *atmo*, which refers to air; *hydro*, which refers to water; and *bio*, which refers to life. The teacher continues instruction on affixes with the words *compose* and *decompose.*
Own	Students relate the vocabulary to observations and everyday happenings of living things in their community (for example, seeing the hawk as a predator who decomposes a squirrel or hearing a weather broadcast talk about atmospheric pressure). Students play the online game Quandary (www.quandarygame.org) to conceptually explore the vocabulary in action.

The following occurs at each tier.

Tier 1: The teacher has students record the vocabulary in their interactive science notebooks with hand-drawn or computer-generated art and a caption that describes each term.

Tier 2: The teacher provides a small group of students with instruction three times each week for thirty minutes on high frequency, multi-meaning vocabulary. He or she offers students increased visual and auditory engagements and text applications.

Tier 3: In addition to the core instruction, the teacher gives these students daily reading skill intervention, increased attention, and more vocabulary resources. Co-teachers collaboratively record students' weekly reading acumens with formative assessments that drive the next week's interventions.

Figure 2.12: Middle school science PRO-vocabulary example.

High School Lesson	SOH-CAH-TOA (sine equals opposite over hypotenuse-cosine equals adjacent over hypotenuse-tangent equals opposite over adjacent)
Prioritize	The teacher begins this trigonometry lesson reviewing the terms *right triangle*, *right angle*, *hypotenuse*, *adjacent*, and *opposite*.
Relate	The teacher shares the Pythagorean theorem definition: The square of the hypotenuse (side opposite the right angle) is equal to the sum of the squares of the other two sides. Then, he or she leads a discussion on the terms *sine*, *cosine*, and *tangent*.
Own	The teacher accesses the Teaching Channel (n.d.) video "Introduction to Trigonometry" (http://bit .ly/2eBJ6Z3), which offers sensory elements to help students own the vocabulary through demonstration. For example, students can spray a mist to indicate the side opposite an angle, and play drums to remember the mnemonic *SOH-CAH-TOA* for the trigonometric functions of sine, cosine, and tangent. Students reinforce vocabulary (*sine equals opposite over hypotenuse*, *cosine equals adjacent over hypotenuse*, and *tangent equals opposite over adjacent*) using low-tech, handheld mathematics vocabulary index cards, along with digital cards that students create and review on Quizlet (https://quizlet.com /4929777/soh-cah-toa-flash-cards).

The following occurs at each tier.

Tier 1: Students and teacher collectively complete an overview of types of triangles on an interactive board. The teacher projects a Flocabulary (2016) printable (http://bit.ly/2emGcrp) for the class, as students label the sides, legs, and hypotenuse in given triangles and solve simple hypotenuse word problems.

Tier 2: The teacher gives this small group of students personalized instruction with increased repetition, application, and reinforcement three times each week for fifty-minute periods.

Tier 3: The school mathematics interventionist provides these students with daily adaptive instructional sessions with additional mathematical skills and practice, targeting and strengthening lower foundational skills.

Figure 2.13: High school trigonometry PRO-vocabulary example.

Conclusion

Through vocabulary, students develop vital critical-thinking skills to internalize concepts while they classify, categorize, relate, and comprehend vocabulary in fictional and informational contexts through oral discussion, comprehension, and written expression. Students must feel connected to the vocabulary in order to own it.

This chapter included lesson examples that value the appropriate interventions to ensure that vocabulary instruction is meaningful. Although it offered specific grade-level lessons, teachers can adapt and apply these strategies and interventions to their own grade levels, curriculum, and of course, students.

The next chapter continues with further exploration of how tiered literacy and mathematics applications honor learner diversity and evidence-based practices.

Phonemic Awareness and Fluency Record

Name: _____

Directions: Record each student's skills by checking off areas of proficiency and highlighting areas that require remediation. Offer assessment dates and comments to use this as a running record and to guide phonemic interventions.

Beginning Skills	Advancing Skills	Fine-Tuning the Skills
☐ Short vowels	☐ Short verse and poems	☐ Phonemic progress (metacognition)
☐ Long vowels	☐ Multisyllabic words	☐ Decoding skills
☐ Consonants	☐ Prefixes and affixes	☐ Encoding skills
☐ Digraphs	☐ Vocabulary	☐ Real words
☐ Diphthongs	☐ Paragraphs	☐ Pseudo words
☐ r-controlled vowels	☐ Word exploration	☐ Syllable instruction
☐ Additional sounds	☐ Words read in fiction	☐ Words-per-minute: _____
☐ Rhyming words	☐ Nonfiction text	☐ Explicit instruction with:
Syllable Segmentation	☐ Other: _____	_____
☐ Sound substitution		_____
☐ Sound isolation		☐ Graph progress
☐ Phonemic segmentation		**Consultation and Collaboration**
☐ Words-per-minute: _____		☐ Reading interventionist
		☐ Speech-language therapist
		☐ General education teacher
		☐ Special education teacher
		☐ Prior teacher
		☐ Colleague
		☐ Family
		☐ Student
		☐ Peers
		☐ Administration
		☐ Additional strategies
		_____
		_____

Additional Student Comments, Data, and Assessments

Comprehension of Fiction, Narrative, and Expository Text

Name: _____

Directions: Record each student's skills by checking off areas of proficiency and highlighting areas that require remediation. Offer assessment dates and comments to use this as a running record and to guide interventions in student comprehension of fiction, narrative, and expository text. Check off the genres and adaptations applied.

Beginning Skills	Advancing Skills	Fine-Tuning the Skills
Fiction	☐ Genre choice	☐ Modeling
☐ Characterization	☐ Paraphrase fiction text	☐ Close reading
☐ Plot	☐ Paraphrase nonfiction text	☐ Examples
☐ Setting	☐ Sequence	☐ Nonexamples
☐ Retelling	☐ Retell	☐ Digital recording
☐ Realistic fiction	☐ Predict	☐ Speech to text
☐ Historical fiction	☐ Make inferences	☐ Detailed explanation
☐ Science fiction	☐ Draw conclusions	☐ Shorter excerpts
☐ Myth	☐ Cite text-based evidence	☐ Discussion
☐ Fantasy	☐ Summarize	☐ Vocabulary
☐ Graphic novel	☐ Annotate	☐ Oral expressions
☐ Short story	☐ Note taking	☐ Organization
☐ Poem	☐ Interactive notebooks	☐ Key features
☐ First-person narrative	☐ Reading journals	☐ Signal words
☐ Third-person narrative	☐ Comparisons	☐ Plot development
Nonfiction	☐ Author's point of view	☐ Text organization
☐ Title	☐ Create own questions	☐ Character actions
☐ Headings	☐ Application	☐ Written expressions
☐ Table of contents	☐ Transfer	☐ Sensory descriptions
☐ Preface	☐ Generalization	☐ Word choice
☐ Index	☐ Classroom centers	☐ Facts
☐ Illustrations	☐ Libraries	☐ Details
☐ Charts	☐ Magazines	☐ Theme
☐ Captions	☐ Newspapers	☐ Whole class
☐ Maps	☐ Cookbooks	☐ Small group
☐ Glossary	☐ How-to-manuals	☐ Remediation
☐ Inform	☐ Online articles	☐ Enrichment
☐ Explain	☐ Independent assignment	☐ One-to-one instruction
☐ Entertain	☐ Cooperative assignment	**Consultation and Collaboration**
☐ Biography	☐ Remediation	☐ Reading interventionist
☐ Memoir	☐ Enrichment	☐ Speech-language therapist
☐ Poem	☐ Multiple engagements	☐ General education teacher
☐ Science article		☐ Special education teacher
☐ News article		☐ Prior teacher
☐ Technical		☐ Colleague
☐ Other: _____		☐ Family
		☐ Student
		☐ Peers
		☐ Administration
		☐ Additional strategies

A–Z Vocabulary List

A	
B	
C	
D	
E	
F	
G	
H	
I	
J	
K	
L	
M	
N	
O	
P	
Q	
R	
S	
T	
U	
V	
W	
X	
Y	
Z	
Select five words to use in a paragraph about _____.	My _____ paragraph:

PRO-Vocabulary Instruction

Name:		
Prioritize Select important words.	**Relate** Cite text that uses the vocabulary.	**Own** Write a sentence with the word. Where else have you seen or heard the word?

CHAPTER 3

CREATING TIERED INTERVENTIONS FOR LITERACY AND MATHEMATICS

Teaching is enhanced when evidence-based practice enters the classroom (Kepes, Bennett, & McDaniel, 2014). Students are not born as readers, writers, or mathematicians; they develop these skills through effective evidence-based instruction. RTI is part of that instruction, informed by the evidence to meet students at their levels of proficiency.

> *Teaching is enhanced when evidence-based practice enters the classroom.*

As previously noted, RTI offers multitiered levels of interventions through a collaborative approach that values early identification, high-quality teaching, and evidence-based instructional strategies (Turse & Albrecht, 2015). The Council for Exceptional Children (2014) writes that evidence-based practice involves well-designed instruction and quality interventions. We must recognize that each student is an individual learner who achieves literacy and mathematics gains at his or her own pace, based on prior knowledge, interest, motivation, effort, and of course, quality instruction. RTI offers a way to deliver the systematic interventions with consistency and high expectations for all students.

Literacy and mathematics are two disciplines that spill over into other subjects, whether one is navigating a website, identifying shapes in artwork, reading the lyrics of a song, solving a scientific equation, or performing a play. Students who do not easily decode the letters in words, comprehend fiction and nonfiction genres, or accurately own the mathematics skills might have difficulties reading fluently, writing effectively, listening to and interpreting directions, speaking with confidence and clarity, and computing and applying the skills to solve simple and more complex mathematics problems.

English and language arts teachers do not own literacy skills; these skills apply across the curriculum. Students can meaningfully strengthen their language arts abilities when they think critically and transfer and apply information across a variety of disciplines. For example, students can share thoughts about a scientific principle with poetry in interactive journals and verbal discussions. Other literacy opportunities might include critiquing a painting, solving a mathematics word problem, singing in a chorus, playing an instrument, or reading about an historical event. English language arts and reading skills exist in every aspect of a student's day as forms of communication, expression, and reflection, whether that form is a song, dance, game, informational article, or persuasive essay.

As discussed in the introduction, RTI offers a multitiered system of supports to address the diverse levels of learners in K–12 classrooms (Buffum, Mattos, & Weber, 2010). These approaches are based on the research of Lev Vygotsky's (1978) principle of the zone of proximal development, which measures the difference between independent tasks that a student can perform without assistance and tasks for which a student requires assistance or scaffolding. The goal is for teachers to reach students on levels where they can experience success toward learning outcomes minus the frustrations that result from inappropriately leveled work.

Figure 3.1 illustrates the structure of this chapter.

The Spectrum

Diversity exists with living and nonliving things, from foods to vehicles to snowflakes to people. Apples are red, green, delicious, golden, tart, and sweet, to name a few characteristics. Chocolate is bitter, sweet, dark, white, milk, and plain; it

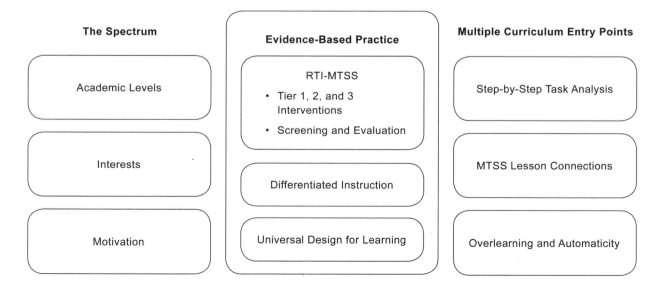

Figure 3.1: Plan for creating tiered interventions for literacy and mathematics.

can have nuts or can coat a pretzel or a raisin. If you are buying a car, you will see variety at the dealership—coups, all-terrain vehicles, trucks, sports cars, luxury vehicles, and hybrids. Not every food has the same taste or characteristics, nor does each car require identical maintenance. Students exist on a spectrum as well, with varying academic levels, interests, and motivations. Embracing this spectrum requires responsive instructional interventions that connect to a diversity of academic levels, student interests, and motivation.

Academic Levels

Students are all different; they process and apply information with nonconformity. They do not look or act the same on the inside or outside. Students with and without IEPs often present diverse reading, writing, and mathematics acumens, along with differing communicative, emotional, social, and behavioral levels.

Teachers, therefore, should organize instruction in a way that inspires *all* students to learn. They can offer presentations that value diverse learner levels and deliver lesson objectives in increments that allow students time to apply the knowledge and practice the skills. This includes provisions for different pacing, materials, and engagements. Teachers must present core instruction differently and allow students to engage with the curriculum in ways that honor their diverse levels and skill sets. At times, some students require alternate and supplemental instruction beyond whole-class lessons in a multitiered environment that recognizes and responds to their individual needs.

A student's baseline level is his or her starting point, or what he or she already knows. This leads to grade-level academic goals and objectives that include critical-thinking skills with functional applications. However, the essential ideas, or

what is sometimes referred to as *takeaways from lessons*, have expanded from knowing how to read, write, and do mathematics to include cultural, visual, oral, digital, and expanded textual literacy (Andrelchik, 2015; Chandler, Fortune, Lovett, & Scherrer, 2016; Hutchison & Colwell, 2014).

> *Teachers should organize instruction in a way that inspires* all *students to learn.*

Students' diverse academic baseline levels must influence teachers' instructional decisions. RTI practices that identify learner levels drive appropriate instructional practices. For example, a student with a specific learning difference, attention deficit hyperactivity disorder (ADHD), or autism may excel when engaged in digital technology, but he or she may also possess differing academic or behavioral levels from the majority of his or her classmates. Therefore, multitiered instruction must engage students with evidence-based interventions designed to strengthen each learner's skills on his or her diverse level of functional achievement within classrooms that accept diversity as the norm.

Interests

Quality schools promote student inquiry with the academics linked to learners' lives (Hasni & Potvin, 2015). In such schools, teachers look for ways to engage students in learning based on their interests and who they are. The Bill and Melinda Gates Foundation (2015) reports that data are a component of personalized learning. Data drive decisions, while student disengagement negates progress. Teachers typically respond to learner levels that academic data reveal, but individual student needs, skills, and interests are also important data.

When a teacher personalizes and acknowledges students' interests in his or her instruction, he or she widens the definition of *knowledge* and teaching is more effective. William M. Chace (2015), English emeritus at Stanford University, purports that often educators who enter the field believe that they need to know everything about their subjects, carefully displaying omniscience in front of their students. As an English teacher, he offered his students information about authors and their writings, but he now describes his primary role as the *oxygen supplier* for students to gain more self-knowledge. Oxygen is an ingredient that permits cellular respiration; our lessons need to do the same, allowing learners to energize, inhale, and exhale the concepts.

> *Oxygen is an ingredient that permits cellular respiration; our lessons need to do the same, allowing learners to energize, inhale, and exhale the concepts.*

Teaching is not about next-day delivery. Students are not Amazon Prime members who order and receive packages of core knowledge. It is not about what we as educators give or deliver but about the learning that students receive, own, and apply. Student interest and buy-in drive the lessons and retention of the lesson's concepts; therefore, instruction must engage learners.

When students believe that what they are doing is important, then that strong motivation and buy-in spur more engagement in learning. Teachers must offer students realistic feedback on their content mastery with a viable plan and the appropriate scaffolding to spur on this learning.

Students and teachers can then visualize a plan for achievement. Developing students' intrinsic motivation and ownership of the learning increases self-confidence despite any challenges, whether these challenges are behavioral, emotional, social, communicative, physical, sensory, or academic. Increased buy-in includes properly leveled instruction with strategies and interventions, such as choice boards, learning contracts, and self-advocacy plans.

When teachers provide differentiated options to students to demonstrate their learning, this inspires student conversations and engagements that tap into learner interests. Depending on students' reading, language, speaking, writing, social, emotional, behavioral, and attention levels, teachers can invite students to independently complete interest surveys or conference families to provide responses. Initiating interest surveys in the beginning of the year, and then revisiting these interests later on, allow teachers, students, and families to connect to learner interests and identify growth. It's even better if assignments are tied to these interests. For example, a writing assignment might focus on descriptive words about a student's favorite sport or movie or perhaps a place he or she has visited or would like to visit; while a mathematics word problem might include favorite singers' or actors' names. The reproducible "Interests and Strengths Questionnaire" (page 59) is an excellent tool for helping teachers find out more about their students.

Nonfiction and fiction reading selections that increase reading comprehension or writing skills might offer music, science, history, and art genres, or have a zombie as a character if that falls under high learner interest. President Theodore Roosevelt summed it up well when he stated, "I am part of everything I have read" (Nobel Peace Laureate Project, n.d., p. 1). This sentiment is applicable to delivering all core knowledge. Students who have strong personal connections to or an interest in the topic or assignment have a stronger motivation to learn.

Motivation

Motivation increases student proficiency, but teachers do not motivate learners—they provide the conditions that stimulate student interest (Sieberer-Nagler, 2016). Proficient learners have automaticity of concepts, but struggling learners often require coaching and additional feedback. It would be magical if automaticity of concepts came as easily as breathing. However, automaticity requires practice and adaptations that ease conceptual navigations.

A student who navigates from class to class does not stop to think about a right or left turn or hesitate over which hallway to walk down. Instead, the student moves with confidence and determination that he or she will arrive at the correct location, the next class. This student probably did not exhibit this confidence the first day or perhaps even the first week of school, but it became automatic after instruction, practice, repetition, and application. A student who struggles is often frustrated by work that is above his or her level of proficiency, not knowing how to automatically take the right steps or demonstrate the skills to effectively navigate reading, writing, or mathematics requirements.

Motivation is intrinsic and extrinsic. Respectively, students light their own fires or need more kindling with external rewards. A student who does the mathematics or reads a book because it is exciting to learn new things displays intrinsic motivation. A student who focuses on the words in a teacher's lecture as *required knowledge* needs more motivation beyond, "I'll listen to this because I have to." Motivation does not lie solely on the students' shoulders but also on teachers' shoulders. Energy, enthusiasm, stimulation, and passion are shared learning dynamics.

> *Motivation does not lie solely on the students' shoulders but also on teachers' shoulders.*

Motivation exists on a spectrum, requiring differentiated instruction and diverse engagements that match learners' diverse academic, social, emotional, and behavioral needs. Motivation in learning is influenced by factors such as relevance, control, choice, challenge, social interaction, anticipated sense of success, need, and novelty. Intrinsic motivation involves taking part in an activity for its own sake, while extrinsic motivation includes participating in an activity as a means to an end (Kayalar, 2016).

Students can experience the excitement of discovery when offered flexible tools and diverse teaching approaches that motivate them to own and experience concepts and skills. Positive and appropriately leveled instruction both challenges and sparks student curiosity to learn more. A teacher might say, "I think this next activity will challenge you to do your best," instead of "Many of you will find this activity frustrating." It's always best to lead with the positive.

Place learning on a pedestal. Increase student ownership of their own learning and the desire to learn. Apply the knowledge and skills outside school walls. If a student asks, "Do I need to know this for the test?," the teacher might respond, "Yes, for life's multiple choices."

To help motivate students, teachers should create opportunities that are timely, intrinsic, active, interesting, organized, and nurturing.

Understanding and supporting students include *motivating* them as well.

Evidence-Based Practice

As a pilot navigates the skies or a ship captain charts his or her course, educators help learners succeed in school by providing the appropriate instruction. Navigating a path for each student includes helping him or her figure out how to develop, use, and refine academic skills. When one writes an argumentative essay, the evidence must support the argument. School decisions are no different. Evidence-based practice consists of high-quality instructional strategies that have proof supporting their effectiveness (U.S. Department of Education, Institute of Educational Sciences, National Center for Education Evaluation and Regional Assistance, 2003).

Teachers should not make instructional decisions without thinking about the evidence to support those decisions. RTI's multitiered approach includes infusing evidence-based interventions to set up the expectations and planning learning outcomes (Lenski, 2011). Teachers using RTI identify barriers to learning and then establish the instructional tiers that include whole-class, small-group, and individualized instruction. The application of these evidence-based practices for screening, evaluation, differentiation, and collaboration is delineated in the following sections.

RTI-MTSS

As defined previously, RTI offers a multitiered system of supports, or MTSS. The terms are complementary, and you will sometimes see them used together as RTI-MTSS (Cunningham, n.d.).

RTI tiers target specific student populations who struggle with attaining the concepts offered in the core instruction.

RTI is not about labels, such as a specific learning disability or emotional disturbance, but about decisions that assist students who are struggling with learning during core instruction. Successful outcomes are not exclusive to students who excel with automaticity during core instruction (Tier 1) but are planned for *all* students within an RTI framework. Vigilant teachers allow for a shift back and forth to other instructional gears beyond Tier 1 whole-class instruction.

Tier 1, 2, and 3 Interventions

Tier 1 addresses whole-class core instruction in which the teacher assesses *all* students and determines which learners require additional interventions. Multitiered models such as RTI require both general and special education teachers to: (1) determine what constitutes appropriate Tier 1 practice and (2) consider the relationship between what occurs in Tiers 2 and 3 and the general education classroom (Blanton, Pugach, & Boveda, 2014). This includes identifying students who are succeeding and those who are struggling.

Tier 1 generally includes whole-class, evidence-based instruction, but it also consists of a combination of whole-class and smaller cooperative peer groups learning core concepts together. Tier 2 involves evidence-based instruction for small, targeted groups working on identified skills that require honing. Tier 2 occurs in the general education classroom or in a pullout setting. Tier 3 involves providing students with more intensive instruction. If students do not make progress in Tier 3, then teachers and related service providers determine whether special education services are warranted and may recommend specific and more intensive evaluation after a set time period of interventions. All three tiers offer validated measurements to gauge student levels, known as progress monitoring of the response to intervention.

RTI focuses on academics but also connects to students' emotional and social domains. If behavioral interventions are warranted, then administration should consider additional professional development and resources, such as providing training to teachers who require more knowledge about social, behavioral, and emotional supports.

> *RTI focuses on academics but also connects to students' emotional and social domains.*

RTI examines how general and special educators continually collaborate, along with additional contributory elements that value the tiered and responsive interventions (Cunningham, n.d.). Collaboration includes input from a speech-language pathologist to increase a learner's articulation of phonemes or how to display increased conversational skills in class discussion. A behavioral interventionist, guidance counselor, school psychologist, social worker, learning consultant, or inclusion coach can offer observations and recommendations. Collaborative decisions encompass the areas of motivation, attention, remediation, or enrichment. General and special education staff must work together as a team to support not only their students but each other as well. Collaborative input is an integral component of tiered interventions.

Generally, schools expect that 80 percent of the student population will reach benchmark criteria with the core instruction in Tier 1 (Metcalf, n.d.). Teachers often revisit core instruction when a significant percent of the students experience

difficulties. Rather than referring learners to Tier 2 instruction, teachers must determine whether delivery and engagement are issues preventing student success. Therefore, the *how* of the instruction influences learner outcomes. Sometimes just tweaking delivery and engagement can help teachers reach students more successfully.

Screening and Evaluation

Implementation requires that teachers receive ongoing supports in their classrooms to help with decisions that involve screening, intervention, documentation, and ongoing curriculum-based assessments. Curriculum does not exist in a vacuum; it is intertwined with individual academic and behavioral levels. Teachers must select assessment and screening instruments that drive the instructional tiers.

The Center on Response to Intervention at AIR (n.d.b) rates assessments for their validity, reliability, and evidence-based practices. Visit goo .gl/Znwdg0 to access the center's screening tools chart. The screening tools featured on this site can help teachers determine proficiencies with phoneme segmentation, nonsense word fluency, rhymes, syllables, oral reading, sentence blending, text comprehension, and mathematics skills. Ratings include whether the evidence on the screenings is convincing, partially convincing, unconvincing, or inadequate. For example, the chart shows that easyCBM receives moderate-high ratings for mathematics, multiple-choice reading comprehension, and vocabulary, as does Discovery Education Predictive Assessment for reading and mathematics. The Observation Survey of Early Literacy Achievement, peer-assisted learning strategies (PALS), and State of Texas Assessments of Academic Readiness (STAAR) indicate convincing evidence that the screening tool accurately offers information to determine student levels and whether students are at risk for reading and mathematics disabilities (Center on Response to Intervention at American Institutes for Research, n.d.b).

Student progress hinges on accurate and reliable information. Assessments can never be generic. "Without good diagnostic information and/or a flexible formative assessment system, our instructional programs and student performance will not improve, and RTI will simply be an alternate route to special education placement" (Lipson, Chomsky-Higgins, & Kanfer, 2011, p. 205).

Assessments should be individualized with reliability and validity that correctly identify student skills and levels to generate the appropriate interventions. This includes timely and accurate screenings and assessments given at set intervals to monitor progress. Assessments should never frustrate students or teachers. The main purpose of assessment, whether or not RTI is in the mix, is to guide instruction, not brand students or penalize teachers for lack of student progress.

Teachers use formative assessments to assess reading and mathematics levels and skills to inform instruction. Marcotte and Hintze (2009) discovered that comprehension measurements combined with oral reading fluency are reliable indicators of student performance on high-stakes, criterion-referenced assessments. Research comparing mathematics performance on formative essay tests versus multiple-choice tests revealed that students with high levels of self-directed learning have better outcomes on essay tests than multiple-choice ones. No differences in mathematics learning outcomes were evidenced if the students had low levels of self-directed learning (Sumantri & Satriani, 2016). This research implies that a behavioral component is connected to achievement and assessment. It is essential, therefore, to not only teach students subjects but to help them with behavioral issues, such as learning to organize and self-direct.

Formative assessment offers timely feedback to monitor student progress, gauge instruction, and form the lesson. This kind of assessment can use low-tech or high-tech strategies. For example, students can offer thumbs-up for *yes* or thumbs-down for *no*, complete exit cards after class, share metacognitive journals, complete a five-question quiz, or share responses to key questions on digital devices using technology tools and apps such as Plickers, Kahoot!, or Quizlet.

Screening offers vital information, with the data shaping instruction and intervention. Screening tools are not exclusive to RTI, but they are helpful for guiding instruction. The assessment data reveal areas in the curriculum in which students may be above grade level as well as where they may have gaps in their skill sets (Franklin-Rohr, 2012). The next three sections discuss screening tools for literacy and language arts, mathematics, and behavior.

Screening Considerations and Tools for Literacy and Language Arts

RTI approaches must be sensitive to developmental differences in language and literacy among students at different ages and grades (International Literacy Association, 2009). Teachers should be knowledgeable about the strategies and interventions that address phonemic awareness, phonics, reading fluency, vocabulary, reading comprehension, and written expression. They should include practices for screening, instruction, and evaluation of student reading and writing needs with multiple evidence-based measurements, such as phonics inventories, graded word lists, and sample passages. Teachers need screening information to gather data to differentiate reading and writing lessons. Gersten et al.'s (2008) guide *Assisting Students Struggling With Reading: Response to Intervention (RtI) and Multi-Tier Intervention in the Primary Grades* offers five recommendations for teachers to assist those students who have reading difficulties.

1. Screen students at the beginning and mid-part of the year, and continue to monitor student progress.

2. Provide differentiated instruction based on assessments with student-based support and scaffolding.

3. Establish small-group intensive systematic instruction three to five times each week with increased student-teacher interaction, reading practice, and feedback.

4. Review the data and monitor student progress at Tier 2 at least once each month to identify program effectiveness.

5. Plan Tier 3 instructional practices for students who require more intensive reading skills after not receiving adequate progress on Tier 2.

Administrators should arrange specific professional development for teachers if teachers require more training on ways to increase student success with phonemic awareness, fluency, or reading comprehension. This often involves an instructional coach, a reading and learning specialist, or a language arts supervisor who models how to screen students and apply reading strategies.

Teachers could also choose to visit other reading classes to see the interventions modeled, participate in in-person or online courses, and attend offsite reading workshops and professional conferences. Multiple approaches to teaching reading and writing skills include, but are not limited to, direct instruction, shared peer reading and writing experiences, a balance of choral and silent sustained reading sessions, and guided practice. Reading and writing skills are required across the curriculum and throughout life; therefore, all tiers need to link literacy to functional applications.

> *Reading and writing skills are required across the curriculum and throughout life.*

Screening tools are available for content areas across the curriculum. For example, screening tools for reading and writing range from informal phonics inventories to curriculum-based, multiple-choice reading-comprehension measurements. These tools determine skills such as letter identification, knowledge of consonant digraphs and short vowels in consonant-vowel-consonant (C-V-C) words, fluency, and comprehension.

Screenings for middle and high school students gauge fluency, comprehension, language skills, and written expression. Identifying and attaching meaning to content-related vocabulary, spelling, and grammar; using context clues; drawing conclusions; and summarizing passages are all skills that must be honed to achieve literacy and language success, no matter what a student's grade level.

Curriculum-based inventories, such as the Developmental Reading Assessment (DRA), identify skills such as how many words a learner accurately reads per minute, patterns of word identification errors, and whether a student correctly identifies and interprets fiction and nonfiction comprehension passages, knowing what is directly stated and what is implied or inferred.

Subtests of formal screening tools, such as the Woodcock Reading Mastery or the Texas Primary Reading Inventory, reveal which students require additional instruction, as well as those who master the literacy and require more challenges rather than remediation. They test skills such as graphophonemic knowledge and phonemic awareness to understand letters, sound-symbol relationships, and spelling patterns. Beginning in grades K–3, they assess listening comprehension, reading accuracy, and comprehension, and book and print awareness. Writing assessments such as the First Steps Writing Map of Development and the Teachers College Reading and Writing Project, diagnose more than spelling, punctuation, and grammar to include organization, structure, vocabulary, elaboration, writing fluency, and editing.

Screening tools are often used to determine which students are at risk of failure if they are not provided with the additional interventions. Screening data reveal information that helps teachers decide on the primary intervention needed for core instruction, types of resources, and required collaboration. Data teams review the screening and assessment data at set intervals to make informed decisions about differently leveled texts, daily practice and monitoring to improve fluency, systematic multisensory phonemic instruction, additional rehearsal, and step-by-step comprehension strategies.

Screening Considerations and Tools for Mathematics

Mathematics interventions address proficiencies with computational fluency, problem solving, and visual representations (Hinton, Flores, & Shippen, 2013). It is essential that mathematics automaticity begins in the early grades and escalates with increasing complexity as students advance from primary to the secondary grades. Teachers should provide motivating, real-life applications that connect to student levels and interests to increase computational and problem-solving skills across

the mathematics domains, such as ratio and proportions, algebra, and geometry.

Gersten and colleagues (2009) offer recommendations that include:

> ➤ Screening and providing interventions to students who are identified as at risk

> ➤ Devoting time to fluent retrieval of arithmetic facts

> ➤ Intervening with visual representations

> ➤ Providing explicit and systematic interventions that offer problem-solving models based on common underlying structures, guided practice, corrective feedback, and cumulative review

Some screening tools include the Math Reasoning Inventory (MRI), which determines mathematics fluency with numeracy skills and concepts, such as number quantities and conceptual reasoning in word problems. The screening and ongoing assessments disclose student knowledge and ease with the core instruction from counting numbers, comparing and contrasting sets of objects, solving one-step to multistep word problems, and demonstrating number sense. Students must own skills with whole numbers, fractions, and decimals; however, screening must first identify proficiency levels. Assessments such as KeyMath-3, Scholastic Math Inventory, and First Steps in Mathematics diagnose areas of need with computation and concepts that include algebra, geometry, measurement, money, probability and statistics, number sense, patterns, relationships, and more.

Screenings determine whether classwide, gradewide, or course-specific learning deficits exist. Data teams use screening data to identify students in need of supplemental support. Teachers should conduct an inventory of student levels at the beginning of the year and repeat it as instruction proceeds to verify mastery of grade-level skills (VanDerHeyden & Allsopp, 2014). Screening helps teachers select mathematics programs that offer supplemental instruction to develop computational and conceptual fluencies and more intensive one-to-one, small-group instruction.

Screening Considerations and Tools for Behavior

If students are not responding to classroom behavioral expectations, teachers must provide interventions, the same way they would with academics. Surveys, observations, and student discipline referrals comprise the data that determine the effectiveness of behavioral interventions for the whole class, small groups, and individual students. Interventions might include a social skills group with the guidance counselor, check-in times with teachers and peers, increased feedback, and student self-monitoring combined with teacher conferencing and more frequent home communication, such as a behavioral report card.

> *If students are not responding to classroom behavioral expectations, teachers must provide interventions, the same way they would with academics.*

Students requiring Tier 3 interventions may warrant a behavior support team with a behavioral interventionist conducting a functional behavioral assessment. General and special education teachers, guidance counselors, case managers, and as warranted, behavioral interventionists outline the necessary focus and intervention intensity for students and their families. The functional behavioral assessment determines the reasons for the behavior, which leads to and drives a behavior intervention plan.

The support team gathers information with a problem-solving approach that reviews behavioral data from a variety of sources, including interviews and observations in several contexts and situations to determine the behavioral antecedents and consequences, replacement behaviors desired, and reinforcement-based strategies.

If an educator never had training with functional behavioral assessment and behavior intervention plans, then additional preparation and support may be necessary, including behavior workshops and professional development sessions in collaboration with other trained staff as mentors. Teachers may consult the Technical Assistance Center on Positive Behavioral Interventions and Supports (www.pbis.org) for additional behavioral insights and research connections for core instruction.

Many screening tools are available to assess behavior. Behavioral screenings are written, verbal, observational, and anecdotal and note the level of responsibility students can handle and their ability to follow classroom discipline and social expectations. Behavioral, social, and emotional screening assessments, such as the Conners Comprehensive Behavior Rating Scales, Functional Analysis Screening Tool, Behavior Rating Inventory of Executive Function, and Children's Depression Inventory, measure skills like task initiation, flexibility, emotional control, response inhibition, and developmentally appropriate behavior.

RTI screening, therefore, involves determining literacy, numeracy, and behavioral skills with accuracy and speed of processing letters, words, longer texts, single and multidigit numbers, and school procedures and responsibilities. Working with other staff, teachers use these screening tools to make reflective decisions focused on multiple interventions for academic and behavioral domains. After teachers identify student levels, they can set up the responsive differentiated interventions that match individual student needs.

Teachers should utilize screening tools at set periods during the school year to identify baseline levels and note an increase or decrease of academic skills and appropriate behaviors. This data-based, problem-solving approach then drives instructional decisions.

Differentiated Instruction

Selecting and managing intervention strategies in RTI can be overwhelming for educators who wear a variety of hats every day. The teacher's goal is to reach learners on levels where they can experience success toward learning outcomes minus the frustrations that result from inappropriately leveled work. Research supports the idea that differentiation helps students with mixed-ability levels (Rock, Gregg, Ellis, & Gable, 2008; Tomlinson, 1999).

Differentiated instruction acknowledges varying types of student engagement, motivational factors, diverse student levels, prior knowledge, and varied student learning styles to honor cultural, linguistic, and cognitive differences (Huebner, 2010). Differentiated instruction ensures that delivery of the core content reaches all levels of learners, from students who are struggling to those who are advanced. All students can achieve at higher levels when differentiation is at the heart of instructional practice. Teachers teach *students*, not subjects. Differentiated instruction provides students with multiple curriculum entry points, learning tasks, and outcomes that address individual learner needs (Watts-Taffe et al., 2012).

Core instruction requires differentiation to acknowledge and appropriately address the diverse background knowledge that individual students display. Differentiation has a broad definition that includes honoring how students learn best by varying the content, process, and product (Tomlinson, 1999). Complexity and engagement often differ. For example, a music teacher might ask some students to offer the names of notes on a staff and ask others whether that note is on a line or space, or perhaps identify the line or space where the note is placed (Darrow, 2015).

> *All students can achieve at higher levels when differentiation is at the heart of instructional practice.*

How teachers organize, maintain, and present differentiated instruction varies. Specific examples include learning centers, game-based learning, scaffolds, cognitive strategies, attention to learning styles with multimodal presentations, and technology.

Access to technology in the classroom varies and depends on district resources and staff willingness to differentiate the delivery and engagement. It can include low-tech or high-tech tools. For example, a younger student might enjoy watching a Starfall video on vowel teams (sheeberi, 2009; www.youtube.com/watch?v=o84ndBQU6vQ), while an older student might enjoy hearing Sal Khan (n.d.) offer a mathematics tutorial on how to express a fraction as a decimal (http://bit.ly/2kpQLcs). Technology offers excellent literacy and language possibilities such as text-speech tools, closed captioning on animated curriculum videos, word prediction tools, and dictation. Students can use online virtual mathematics manipulatives (www.illuminations.nctm.org) or may prefer to manipulate a low-tech tool, such as an abacus, to learn place value.

Differentiated instruction requires the collaboration of general and special education teachers, reading and mathematics specialists, coaches, instructional assistants, learning and behavioral specialists, related service providers, and administrators who design, direct, and organize the multitiered structures. A shared vision requires common goals for language and literacy instruction and assessment. This includes adequate time for communication and coordinated planning between general educators and specialist teachers, along with integrated professional development (ILA, 2009). Students' families might also be involved in the collaboration in planning and ongoing decisions about their children. Simply put, having more hands on deck helps to ensure that the core navigation follows a course that addresses each student's learning styles and needs.

Universal Design for Learning

Universal design for learning builds on research from neuroscience, cognitive psychology, and learning sciences (Center for Applied and Special Technology, 2011). UDL is similar to differentiated instruction in the way it acknowledges that students learn differently; however, differentiated instruction decisions are often based on individualized and small-group strategies. UDL propagates a proactive approach, expecting students with diverse skills and abilities to navigate core instruction in Tier 1 by offering multiple representations, engagements, actions, and expressions (National Center on Universal Design for Learning, 2014). Both universal design for learning and differentiated instruction have similar outcomes, which is to reduce learner barriers, increase student skills, and allow students to achieve the lesson outcomes.

With UDL, teachers design goals, methods, materials, and assessments at the onset to reach a wide range of students. The goal is to reduce

barriers in instruction; provide appropriate accommodations, supports, and challenges; and maintain high achievement expectations (Basham, Israel, Graden, Poth, & Winston, 2010). Teachers then offer multitiered instruction with accessibility that is further individualized. For example, a teacher might offer a student in Tier 1 core instruction who is unable to read a grade-level text independently an alternate audio text. If the student requires more time to practice fluency, he or she can accomplish that in Tier 2. If the student is still struggling, the teacher might offer the student an abridged version of the text with lower-level vocabulary and more comprehension supports.

Data from formative assessments and progress monitoring reveal the need for more or less practice and engagement. For Tier 3 instruction, teachers might give students an alternate reading level designed to allow them to engage with the text on a level that increases achievement, minus the frustration.

Support might include offering visual, auditory, and kinesthetic/tactile engagements, along with individual choice and autonomy, which optimize relevance. Teachers can build learner fluency in skills using multiple tools, resources, and technologies, along with graduated supports and ongoing feedback for practice and performance. They must consider not only the core curriculum's substance or content but, most important, how to deliver content. When creating flexible and appropriate tasks, teachers consider prior experiences, background knowledge, interests, and learner strengths.

The diverse levels of students in our classrooms require academic and behavioral adaptations and challenges that offer instructional materials and supports for students who are low performing and high performing. UDL has a crucial role within the RTI framework, which allows all students to arrive at the same destination and achieve literacy and mathematics achievements. Navigation is never a race, but a collaborative process that teachers and supporting staff proactively plan together. When teachers navigate the core curriculum, it is vital to remember to be responsive to each and every student. UDL is an excellent vehicle that allows for this differentiation.

> *Navigation is never a race, but a collaborative process that teachers and supporting staff proactively plan together.*

Multiple Curriculum Entry Points

Multiple curriculum entry points acknowledge that each student is unique and enters the curriculum based on his or her academic, social, emotional, and behavioral baseline levels, which are the starting point for instruction. Multiple entry points value diverse representations, engagements, actions, and expressions that honor learner diversity.

Step-by-Step Task Analysis

Teachers establish RTI through a detailed itinerary and time frame, plotting each turn, step, or connection at a time. This step-by-step approach applies across the curriculum, including literacy, language arts, and mathematics. Each situation requires looking at the lay of the land and then figuring out the route. In reference to lessons, this involves interdisciplinary connections, differentiated instruction, and curriculum-based assessments.

If a student cannot learn a concept, then the teacher must analyze and evaluate each step of the lesson to determine which part of the instruction should be revised to ensure learning. For example, if a student has difficulty reading a history or science text, but has excellent conceptual knowledge, the teacher might arrange to have text read aloud on a digital online site. If a student has good multiplication skills but weaker perceptual skills, then he or she may require cue cards or a calculator to multiply two-digit numbers, or columned paper to line up numbers, to accurately calculate the product.

MTSS Lesson Connections

The lessons in this chapter infuse critical-thinking skills to increase oral expression, listening comprehension, fluency, vocabulary, reading comprehension, written expression, and mathematics knowledge across genres and disciplines. These lessons also offer appropriate supports with multitiered accommodations and modifications for core reading, writing, and mathematics skills. Teachers can implement whole-class, small-group, and one-to-one groupings and at times, pullout instruction. The lessons offer review time with on-level, challenging assignments to prevent misconceptions from escalating or inappropriately leveled work from leading to off-task and improper student behaviors. Lessons and activities that are either too easy or too hard often result in bored or frustrated students who express their inattention through inappropriate behaviors.

> *Lessons and activities that are either too easy or too hard often result in bored or frustrated students.*

Lessons must offer the appropriate interventions, accommodations, and modifications for students to achieve success with core instruction. These lessons model how to incorporate listening comprehension, fluency, vocabulary, reading comprehension, and written expression. They should take place over a period of days to allow for more application, rather than being crammed into a class period.

The reproducible "Tiered UDL-MTSS Literacy Planner" (pages 60–61) offers a template to help design a multitiered lesson that connects the core knowledge to a choice of anticipatory sets, collaborative instructional practices, and professional resources, while valuing scaffolding, enrichment, follow-ups, and most important—diverse student populations. Although teachers are often anxious to get to the "meat" of a lesson, the anticipatory set cannot be ignored, since this is the hook that activates prior knowledge and grabs students' attention.

> *The anticipatory set cannot be ignored, since this is the hook that activates prior knowledge and grabs students' attention.*

The tiered lessons in figures 3.2–3.4 (pages 53–57) include instructional strategies, procedures, and objectives. Student core levels, interests, and motivations are connected through a movie, poem, and historical documents for students in elementary, middle school, and high school. (Visit **go.SolutionTree.com/RTI** to access more free reproducible lesson examples.)

Instructional Strategies, Procedures, and Objectives	**Elementary Lesson** Students extract the elements of a story to gain speaking, listening, oral fluency, reading comprehension, and writing skills with a step-by-step analysis of the movie *Frozen*.	
Tier 1	Students view the movie *Frozen* over a period of three days, analyzing the settings, events, and characters as they unfold. The teacher incorporates the following concepts in science class with a discussion of the weather changes. • **Oral expression:** The teacher initiates a cooperative discussion of the theme. Students assume character roles to retell the story (for example, Anna, Elsa, Kristoff, Sven, Olaf). After viewing the movie, he or she divides the class into Anna and Elsa groups to discuss how the sisters are alike and different. The teacher records students' thoughts and ideas in a Venn diagram posted on the wall to model for students. Based on the collaborative Venn diagram, students write on a compare-and-contrast chart independently or in small groups, which they can use later as a writing planner. • **Listening comprehension:** Students retell the movie's plot with a quiz on the sequence of events. • **Fluency:** Partners orally read a teacher-created passage on *Frozen*. • **Vocabulary:** Students review synonyms and antonyms (for example, *conceal* and *reveal*, *limits* and *limitless*, *fear* and *fearless*, *power* and *weakness*) on flash cards. • **Reading comprehension:** Students review the website Common Sense Media (n.d.; http://bit.ly/2dOLwyP), which contains student reviews of the movie. Students can add their own reviews to the page. Next, students share their *Frozen* reviews with peers. • **Written expression:** Students write concrete poems in the shapes of snowflakes.	

Figure 3.2: Grades 2–3 language arts lesson on *Frozen*.

Tier 2	The teacher offers some students story frames with the prompts *first*, *next*, *later*, *after*, and *finally*. He or she provides instruction three times each week to organize students' verbal and written expressions, offers students with further modeling and practice, and gives students with fine motor difficulties snowflake templates for their concrete poems as the instructional assistant helps with teacher guidance and monitoring.			
Tier 3	The reading specialist reviews different vocabulary and reading levels for the passages during small-group instruction four times each week for fifty-minute periods.			
Anticipatory Set	Students listen to the song "Let It Go" (Anderson-Lopez & Lopez, 2013).			
Assessments	Students participate in cloze reading exercises, vocabulary quizzes, performance-based discussion responses, movie critiques, and concrete snowflake poem writing.			
Resources	The teacher activates visual and auditory elements with closed captioning on as students view and listen to the movie. He or she has students move to classroom art, music, and performance centers to work in groups. The teacher asks students to decorate their snowflakes with 3-D art materials, explore the lyrics of songs, and reenact movie scenes.			
Collaboration	Collaboration takes place with the music and art teachers' input for the snowflake project and exploration of the stanzas in "Let It Go."			
Tiered Scaffolding: Multitiered Accommodations or Modifications (for diverse levels and skill sets)	Students complete lesson skill requirements (ranges from partial to full participation)	☑ With accommodations □ With modifications	□ With a parallel or related assignment or task	**Additional comments or supports regarding accommodations, modifications, and proficiency levels (include enrichment and remediation):** Follow-up plans for enrichment and remediation include performance-based assessments to guide future reading and writing instruction.
Additional Resources	• ReadWriteThink (2012): Theme poems page: http://bit.ly/2kniqvW • e-Learning for Kids' science and weather page: www.e-learningforkids .org/science/lesson/weather			

Instructional Strategies, Procedures, and Objectives	**Middle School Lesson** Students analyze the Edgar Allan Poe (1845) poem "The Raven" and cite text-based evidence that supports what the poem states and implies.
Tier 1	• **Oral expression:** Students share the ideas Poe expresses in Socratic discussion, using appropriate syntactic, pragmatic, and semantic language structures to analyze the words, sentences, and text meaning. • **Listening comprehension:** Students extract important information from digital reads of the poem. • **Fluency:** Students recite the poem to a peer, producing the appropriate rhyming patterns and pauses.

	• **Vocabulary:** Students sort the poem's vocabulary into categories of nouns (*raven, countenance*), verbs (*pondered, marveled*), adjectives (*quaint, silken*), and adverbs (*ghastly, nevermore*) on color-coded index cards. • **Reading comprehension:** Students answer specific written questions on a hierarchy of complexity (for example, How does the narrator respond to the sound he hears? What does the raven symbolize?) • **Written expression:** Students write a poem in a different setting using a narrative format to convey an emotion.
Tier 2	Adjust the pacing for three students with learning differences. Break down the eighteen stanzas across three dates, reading six stanzas each day, with a co-teacher offering guided instruction and more frequent checks for understanding.
Tier 3	Two students read a graphic novel of the poem and practice fluency with graded sight words within a separate setting. Provide additional daily forty-minute reading instruction in both the classroom and a pullout setting. Teachers can use the following professional resources to support the lesson. Review these websites to gain more information on ADHD and specific learning disabilities. • ADDitude: Strategies and Support for ADHD and LD (2016): www.additudemag.com/index.html • Understood for Learning and Attention Issues' "Understanding ADHD" (Morin, n.d.): http://u.org/1gtcwnV
Anticipatory Set	Students compare and contrast two videos depicting the poem: • *Edgar Allan Poe, The Raven, Read by James Earl Jones* (Beyond the Darkness Publications, 2010): www.youtube.com/watch?v=WcqPQXqQXzl • *The Simpsons: Edgar Allan Poe—The Raven* (Gongadze, 2011): www.youtube.com/watch?v=bLiXjaPqSyY
Assessments	The teacher grades students on class discussion, written and oral responses, morphology of parts of speech sorted, and poems created.
Resources	Digital platforms with visual and audio stimuli
Collaboration	Following the whole-class lesson, students form small groups to discuss the terms *setting, mood, imagery,* and *symbolism.*

Tiered Scaffolding: Multitiered Accommodations or Modifications (for diverse levels and skill sets)	Students complete lesson skill requirements independently (full participation)	☑ With accommodations	☑ With modifications	☐ With a parallel or related assignment or task	**Additional comments or supports regarding accommodations, modifications, and proficiency levels (include enrichment and remediation):** The teacher assesses learner background information and offers prior knowledge about Edgar Allan Poe to the class so students can better understand his motivation for writing the poem. Students review Poe's literary devices in the interactive video TeachersFirst: The Raven (http://teachersfirst.com/lessons/raven/start-fl.cfm). The teacher offers any students with ADHD frequent movement breaks during the lesson.
Additional Resources	American Masters' (2006) series about Edgar Allan Poe on PBS: http://to.pbs.org/2ehfXOQ				

Figure 3.3: Grade 7 language arts lesson on the "The Raven."

Instructional Strategies, Procedures, and Objectives	**High School Lesson** Students analyze and discuss primary documents to gain core knowledge of African American history.

Tier 1	Students jigsaw documents (A–H) to reference African American history. In a jigsaw, students break out into small groups to explore the documents. They then form different groups to discuss specific aspects of those documents. Afterward, they return to their original groups to share what they learned. Students answer document-based questions, make inferences, and formulate perspectives. Students gain knowledge in discussion, presentations, annotated time lines, and argumentative writings.
	
	    A. Louisiana's Code Noir (1724)
	    B. Constitution of the Female Anti-Slavery Society of Salem (1832)
	    C. *United States v. The Amistad* (1841)
	    D. The Fugitive Slave Act (1850)
	    E. The Civil Rights Act of 1875
	    F. Executive Order 8802 (1941)
	    G. *Brown v. Board of Education of Topeka* (1954)
	    H. The Civil Rights Act of 1964
	
	• **Oral expression:** Students discuss appropriate word choice and sentence fluency that clearly state and organize the ideas gained from the primary documents.
	• **Listening comprehension:** Students listen to videos of the documents to identify point of view (for example, Brown v. Board of Education [History, n.d.a] at http://bit.ly/1FGmydr).
	• **Fluency:** Students cite document excerpts with appropriate tone, voice, and expression.
	• **Vocabulary:** Students examine and justify the meaning of document-based vocabulary using the words in the context of passages, speeches, and legislation (for example, applying reading skills such as cause and effect, conclusion, analysis, evidence, inference, prediction, summarization, and salient points).
	• **Reading comprehension:** Students participate in cloze reading, which includes reading and rereading as the words unfold to understand and organize document ideas. Students then record responses, using annotated notes and sticky notes.
	• **Written expression:** Students create an argumentative, five-paragraph essay with details from one of the documents.

Tier 2	Students with differing background knowledge do multiple reads with increased feedback. Students use Cornell Notes (Learning Toolbox, n.d.) to extract the text evidence in the documents. Cornell Notes organize each section's main idea in the text, and then offer more explanation in another area on the page. The co-teacher instructs students three times each week for forty-five-minute periods.
Tier 3	The teacher offers two students shorter text pieces to gain ideas on how to use cloze reading in small-group instruction. The teacher then gives students writing frames that include step-by-step instructions and daily checks for essay editing and revising. Finally, the teacher provides additional reading comprehension strategies with weekly progress monitoring that offer reading and writing interventions and techniques.
Anticipatory Set	The teacher shows the class a document-based question time line and gives students instructions to jigsaw the letters in cooperative groups to collectively research specific details. A 1724 › B 1832 › C 1841 › D 1850 › E 1875 › F 1941 › G 1954 › H 1964 ›
Assessments	Authentic assessments based on these documents include text-based questions, essays, time lines, class discussions, presentations, and student conferencing.

Resources	Students view videos, examine online sources, and listen to recordings of these documents. They review the National Archives and activate the text-to-speech feature at Research Our Records (www.archives.gov/research). Students research other visual text to understand more about these concepts (for example, Salem State College [n.d.; http://landmark.salemstate.edu/fugitive_visual_texts.html]).				
Collaboration	Students edit and revise each other's essays and collectively include facts on the time line. The teacher offers short lessons to the whole class and smaller groups on how to cite sources and identify credible websites, such as OWL resources from the Purdue Online Writing Lab (https://owl.english.purdue.edu) (Weida & Stolley, 2013).				
Tiered Scaffolding: Multitiered Accommodations or Modifications (for diverse levels and skill sets)	Students complete lesson skill requirements independently (full participation)	☑ With accommodations	☑ With modifications	☐ With a parallel or related assignment or task	Additional comments or supports regarding accommodations, modifications, and proficiency levels (include enrichment and remediation): Assignments on primary sources from Library of Congress's (n.d.b) "Teacher's Guides and Analysis Tool" (http://bit.ly/1gICTBw)
Additional Resources	• American Speech-Language-Hearing Association's Typical Speech and Language Development: www.asha.org/public/speech/development • "Using Document-Based Questions With Struggling Readers" (Teachinghistory.org, 2016): http://teachinghistory.org/teaching-materials/ask-a-master-teacher/14958 • The DBQ Project: www.dbqproject.com • "African American History: Primary Documents" (BlackPast.org, 2015): www.blackpast.org/african-american-history-primary-documents				

Figure 3.4: Grade 10 American history lesson on African American history.

These lessons note big ideas that are the core knowledge. These are enduring ideas, not the minor details. Big ideas are higher-level critical-thinking skills; they promote synthesizing and applying the concepts. For example, asking a student to identify the date that Christopher Columbus landed in the New World is not tapping into a student's knowledge of the big ideas. However, asking the student to explain the effect that Europeans' arrival had on Native American culture is an essential or big idea question.

Grant Wiggins and Jay McTighe (2011) emphasize that lessons should examine the core concepts and desired outcomes at the onset, with the evidence or assessments as the next stage of lesson planning, instructional activities, and experiences.

Overlearning and Automaticity

Mathematics, reading, writing, and language skills across the curriculum require overlearning and automaticity. Teachers must design and present core concepts and skills in a way that students in each grade and discipline embrace, retain, apply, and own. Practice, repetition, and diverse engagement allow students to "play" with the concepts in a way that encourages ownership. If teachers offer students the opportunity to overlearn something, then students learn to perform the skill proficiently, automatically, unhesitatingly, and masterfully.

As this chapter's lessons show, scaffolding does not dilute the learning demands but offers a gradual increase of access to grade-level core curricula with the appropriate support systems. Students often require overlearning to develop automaticity, and teachers need time to plan and reflect on how to continually infuse the skills within a tiered instructional model.

> *Scaffolding does not dilute the learning demands but offers a gradual increase of access to grade-level core curricula with the appropriate support systems.*

The reproducible "Lesson-Planning Template: Learner Outcomes and Skills" (pages 62–63) is a template for designing lessons. It helps teachers outline lesson objectives and skills. Whether they are teaching a lesson on a poem, tall tale, science article, or primary document or navigating a mathematics website, teachers must proactively plan instructional strategies, procedures, and objectives, along with the anticipatory sets, assessments, professional resources, scaffolding, and opportunities to offer differentiation for enrichment and repetition of skills.

Conclusion

As highlighted in this chapter, each student presents a diverse baseline level of core knowledge, along with varying interests and motivations. Varying learner levels affect reading, writing, language, and mathematics performances, along with achievements in other disciplines and school navigations. RTI addresses learner diversity with whole-class, small-group, and individualized instruction, as trained staff use the tiered instructional model to deliver the appropriate engagements, resources, and scaffolding. Evidence-based practices of differentiated instruction and universal design for learning support RTI through a collaborative, problem-solving approach that monitors student progress.

Teachers and support staff work together as collaborative teams to review student performance and implement step-by-step task analysis to determine which students require repetition or enrichment. Multitiered instruction across the disciplines can hone students' skills, knowledge, and strategic fluencies in both academics and behavior. This instruction must include opportunities for students to practice and apply skills both inside and outside the classroom.

Interests and Strengths Questionnaire

What I like about myself and others:
What I'd change about myself and others:
Favorite subjects and activities:
Least favorite subjects and activities:
Best friends:
Songs, books, and movies I like:
A job that I might like to do one day:
Skills that would help me to do that job:
What might stop me from doing what I want (people, my weaknesses):
Who could help me achieve my goals:
Other things I think about:

Tiered UDL-MTSS Literacy Planner

Subjects: _____ Units: _____

Themes: _____ Topics or concepts: _____

Skills: _____ Learning standards or goals: _____

Outcomes: _____

Tier 1 includes all students, but list the names of the students that need Tier 2 and 3 support, once determined.

Tier 2: _____

Tier 3: _____

Check all that apply.
Reading skills:

☐ Print concepts (reading left to right, top to bottom, text features, fiction, nonfiction)
☐ Phonemic awareness (working with individual sounds in words)
☐ Phonics (learning to read and write sounds in words)
☐ Fluency (accuracy, speed, expression)
☐ Vocabulary (academic, discipline specific, school or life-related word meaning)
☐ Word decoding (sounding out unfamiliar words with phonics, patterns, structural analysis)
☐ Sight-word recognition
☐ Syllable instruction (closed, open, Vowel-Consonant-*e*, vowel team, consonant-*le*, *r*-controlled)
☐ Morphology (word parts: prefixes, suffixes, base words)
☐ Spelling (encoding skills)
☐ Written expression (meaningful phrases, grammar, sentence formation, organization, paragraphs, essays, poems)
☐ Comprehension skills (author's purpose, main idea, supporting details, sequencing, cause and effect, context clues, characterization, setting, plot, compare and contrast, drawing conclusions, literary elements, fact or opinion, point of view, summarizing, making connections, inferential skills)

Student personalization: levels, strengths, challenges, interests (visual, auditory, and kinesthetic/tactile)

Student connection of UDL principles for reading instruction and assessment:

page 1 of 2

a. Multiple means of representation reading options (prior knowledge, transfer, generalization, vocabulary, multiple media)

b. Multiple means of action or expression reading options (planning, strategy development, goal setting, response, technologies)

c. Multiple means of engagement reading options (motivation, reflection, feedback, choice, empowerment, relevance)

Collaborative reading partners (students, families, administration, co-teachers, instructional assistants, speech-language pathologist, occupational therapist, physical therapist, and other related service providers):

Progress monitoring notes:

Reading reflections and moving forward:

Lesson-Planning Template:
Learner Outcomes and Skills

Instructional Strategies, Procedures, and Objectives	
Tier 1	• Oral expression: • Listening comprehension: • Fluency: • Vocabulary: • Reading comprehension: • Written expression:
Tier 2	
Tier 3	

Anticipatory Set	
Assessments	
Resources	
Collaboration	

Tiered Scaffolding: Multitiered Accommodations or Modifications (for diverse levels and skill sets)	Students complete lesson skill requirements (ranges from partial to full participation)	☐ With accommodations	☐ With modifications	☐ With a parallel or related assignment or task	Additional comments or supports regarding accommodations, modifications, and proficiency levels (include enrichment and remediation)
Additional Resources	Teachers can use the following resources (books, journals, or websites) to support the lesson.				

CHAPTER 4

IMPLEMENTING BEST PRACTICES

Some people in education speak about leveling the playing field, but this term is often open to broad interpretation. If all students do not begin at the same point in terms of their skills, levels, and interests, then the field should be constructed differently. Not all students are able to read, write, complete mathematics problems, or behave with high levels of proficiency at the onset of the school year. The intention of best practices is to offer all students opportunities to learn with proactive differentiated strategies that value what research says about how students learn best.

Identical mastery and progress are myths for our population of diverse learners. Therefore, a multitiered system of supports assists learners to achieve academic and behavioral strides. Students are the data that staff review. Differentiated instruction and universal design for learning acknowledge the merits of offering students multiple access points to the concepts. This chapter's takeaways include varying engagements, representations, actions, and expressions that allow students to achieve success.

> *Identical mastery and progress are myths for our population of diverse learners.*

Teachers must begin, continue, and then fine-tune learning experiences based on how students respond to interventions. They must personalize the learning experience by monitoring each student's progress, effort, and mastery of the concepts. Literacy, mathematics, and behavioral concepts and skills are obtainable through multiple curriculum entry points that value the connections to other subjects and the necessary accommodations and modifications.

This chapter demonstrates how diverse approaches and subject connections honor *all* students, including those who require multiple exposures to the subject matter. Cross-curricular and personal connections are essential for students at all levels. The chapter concludes with lessons that offer tiered, cross-curricular connections and the multitiered system of supports that embraces best practices. Figure 4.1 illustrates the structure of this chapter.

The Big Ideas

Grant Wiggins (2010) writes that an idea is *big* if it helps make sense of a lot of seemingly isolated facts and confusing experiences. The big ideas in literacy are the themes because they provide the mental schemas or templates. If a student lacks phonological awareness or the motivation to read, then he or she will never understand the big idea without additional interventions.

In mathematics, the big ideas, as Charles (2005) defines them, are statements that are central to the learning of mathematics, those that link numerous mathematical understandings into a coherent whole. Mathematics is a diverse discipline that includes having number sense; an understanding of symbols, shapes, and patterns; and performing simple computations and understanding algorithms. We cannot expect students to perform

given mathematics requirements if they do not have a grasp of the foundational core ideas.

Literacy and Mathematics Achievements

We cannot infuse instructional practices that increase literacy and mathematics achievements with the blink of a pedagogical eye. There are no quick fixes to remediate areas such as oral expression, listening comprehension, literacy, and mathematical skills. Students need to view and own reading, writing, and mathematics as passions, not disciplines. Reading fluency, reading comprehension, vocabulary development, written expression, mathematical calculation, and problem-solving skills are requirements across the curriculum and in life. Systematic evidence-based practice fuels these skills.

Literacy involves not only reading the text but also understanding *how* to read the text. This is a skill students can apply across disciplines and genres. Students who are able to accurately

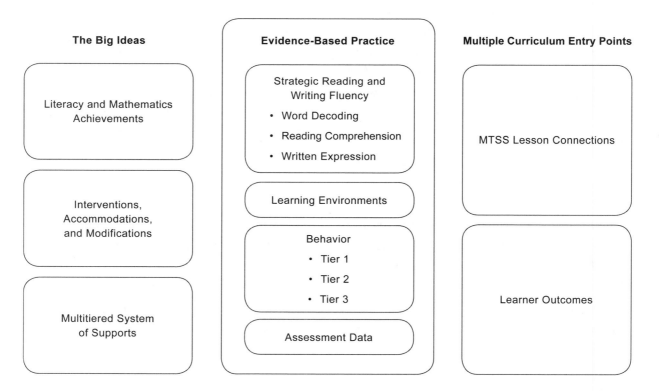

Figure 4.1: Plan for implementing best practices.

decode do not always accurately comprehend. Instruction on how to read a nonfiction article, mathematics word problem, or historical document helps students access the big ideas. Rapidly reading text without processing what the words are saying is a waste of time. It is also vital to address the skill sets of students who have poor fluency and word attack skills but possess excellent comprehension skills.

> *Literacy involves not only reading the text but also understanding* how *to read the text.*

A literate student:

- ➢ Decodes
- ➢ Encodes
- ➢ Previews
- ➢ Listens
- ➢ Reads
- ➢ Expresses
- ➢ Thinks
- ➢ Cares
- ➢ Researches
- ➢ Writes
- ➢ Shares
- ➢ Applies
- ➢ Compares
- ➢ Contrasts
- ➢ Analyzes
- ➢ Questions
- ➢ Critiques
- ➢ Evaluates
- ➢ Connects
- ➢ Collaborates
- ➢ Personalizes
- ➢ Owns

Students are not born literate; they develop literacy skills over time. They own and apply what they learn in school to their lives as they continue from elementary to middle school to high school. This includes metacognition with increased error analysis and feedback. Reading obstacles exist, but so do the strategies to overcome those barriers. Everything is a process, especially writing, which like many other disciplines cannot be separated from critical-thinking skills.

Evidence suggests that explicitly teaching appropriate writing strategies using a model-practice-reflect instructional cycle is an effective way for secondary students to improve their writing (Graham et al., 2016). This includes modeling how to plan, organize, edit, and revise written expressions, whether the student is writing a descriptive, narrative, informative, or persuasive essay or a blog.

Content-area literacy—the ability to use listening, speaking, reading, writing, and viewing—is required to gain information within a specific discipline (Vacca, Vacca, & Mraz, 2010). Teachers who are experts in their own disciplines require additional professional development tools to acquire expertise as readers, writers, and critical thinkers, regardless of the subject matter they teach. For example, a mathematics teacher should be aware of the student who knows the mathematics but has difficulty reading a word problem, while the science teacher might need to assist a student to accurately read step-by-step lab instructions to perform an experiment (Schoenbach, Greenleaf, & Hale, 2010).

Interventions, Accommodations, and Modifications

Appropriate interventions, accommodations, and modifications connect students to core instruction through differentiated, whole-class strategies and tiered lessons. Both accommodations and modifications are types of adaptations that the teacher applies through whole-class, small-group, and individualized instruction. Accommodations generally do not alter the learning outcomes or expectations, while modifications most often change the complexity and the content or what a student is expected to achieve.

For example, a student who listens to a digital version of a social studies passage to answer the same questions as his or her classmates is receiving an accommodation that alters how he or she accesses the content, not a modification of the expectations. However, that is a modification, if the student listens to the text and only highlights the people or dates. If a mathematics student solves one-step word problems, while his or her classmates solve multistep word problems, then that would be a modification.

Changing the *what* and *how* of learning varies according to diverse learner levels. Successes with the core require that students make additional stops before they reach their final destination. Achieving knowledge is a process that necessitates the use of accommodations and modifications, depending on students' skills, prior learning experiences, interests, motivations, and academic levels.

Some students require interventions with basic literacy and mathematics skills. Before they delve into more complex text, students must identify basic terms and phrases such as *title, author, paragraph, chapter, caption, table of contents, index,* and more. The reproducible "Parts of a Book" (page 86) provides a template students can use to identify the different parts of a book during a reading lesson. Content vocabulary is also an important literacy skill. However, some students have more or less prior knowledge. Introducing vocabulary words at the onset then allows introduction and reinforcement. If some students need more modeling, the teacher can intervene with small-group minilessons, while other students independently or cooperatively refine and expand their knowledge.

Students must master content vocabularies in order to achieve academic competencies (Jetton & Alexander, 2004). For example, geography terms are usually organized into a hierarchy, such as *communities, cities, states, countries, continents,* and *hemispheres,* while English terms include

figurative language such as *simile, metaphor, idiom, assonance, hyperbole, alliteration, personification,* and *onomatopoeia.* Teachers should determine if students can understand and decipher the basic academic vocabulary before the content spirals into more complex material. As discussed in chapter 2, vocabulary instruction sometimes requires repetition and enrichment.

Teachers can accommodate and modify lessons to help students achieve ongoing strides with text fluency and comprehension. Even when students receive modifications, the goal is to then fade support to create independent and resilient students who master the core.

In several coaching sessions on both elementary and secondary levels, some educators expressed their hesitation to offer adaptations, whether they were accommodations or modifications. They claimed that accommodations and modifications enable students and create dependency. That is a concern if progress monitoring does not set up a plan to decrease or fade support. The danger of never using adaptations is to create disengaged students who do not care about achieving because they are so familiar with failure. Smaller successes then lead to continuing motivation to achieve.

The reproducibles "Syllable Types" (page 87), "Words and Questions Chart" (page 88), "People, Places, and Things Chart" (page 89), and "Record of Mathematics Skills, Concepts, and Engagements" (page 90) cover some of the big ideas for literacy and mathematics since many students often miss out or cannot extract learning expectations, whether reading a word, sentence, paragraph, or novel or solving a mathematics problem. Teachers can use these organizers to keep track of which skills require more adaptations and to document student progress to inform structured practice.

Multitiered System of Supports

MTSS acknowledges that learners need diverse steps to acquire and then master skills (Haring, Lovitt, Eaton, & Hansen, 1978; Wright, 2013b). Integrating academic and behavioral skills into students' everyday practices is the goal. Mastery occurs in increments, or steps. Teachers must consider how to deliver instruction based on factors such as student levels and the content's complexity.

Some students require more, less, or no help. No one is born fluent in reading, writing, and mathematics skills. Students only learn to apply these skills through instructional practices and experiences that value individual and responsive supports.

> *No one is born fluent in reading, writing, and mathematics skills. Students only learn to apply these skills through instructional practices and experiences that value individual and responsive supports.*

MTSS helps students achieve higher levels of automaticity to absorb, manipulate, and apply symbol-based information. Shapes, letters, words, sentences, and numbers are the building blocks that allow students to understand, own, and apply concepts. We expect all students to achieve the academic core knowledge, yet all students are unique and require differentiated levels of support.

While visiting Athens, Greece, I was surprised to see scaffolding and cranes in front of the Parthenon. The scaffolding of this 2,500-year-old temple was necessary; no one debated about whether scaffolding was needed. The scaffolding did not alter my awe at the structure's magnificence, nor did it skew my sense of the restoration that would follow.

The reproducible "Record of Student Participation" (page 91) can help teachers document student participation, noting the accommodations, modifications, and the parallel activities required to increase student growth. Teachers can use this chart to record how students fare with given activities within a lesson. A mutitiered system of supports allows teachers, students, and families realistic and ongoing information about the degree of lesson participation and scaffolding required. Teachers can evaluate the involvement and instructional supports to develop plans for moving forward.

Evidence-Based Practice

Students may experience challenges as they read, write, compute, and apply knowledge and skills, but they also need to know that they can strategically employ evidence-based strategies. The multitiered instruction within the RTI framework addresses these difficulties. The key is that best practice lives and breathes in classrooms and students' repertoires. For example, text complexity requires that students know how to employ diverse strategies to read a variety of materials. An effective strategy might involve having students practice vocabulary that is slightly above their instructional reading level to increase reading fluency and comprehension (Coulter & Lambert, 2015).

Cross-curricular lessons stimulate higher levels of thinking since connections are made in different areas of the brain that store information for the interrelated subjects, as students learn patterns and skills, not just facts (Willis, 2006). The lessons featured later in this chapter (pages 79–83) model these cross-curricular connections. In the following sections, we will explore four aspects of evidence-based instruction: strategic reading and writing fluency, learning environments, behavior, and assessment data.

Strategic Reading and Writing Fluency

Strategically fluent students go beyond surface-level reading to increase their awareness of how they read (Guerin & Murphy, 2015). This metacognition includes using strategies to improve reading skills. For example, students read a passage once and then reread the passage if they do not understand the text. Teachers must remind students to look up unfamiliar words in a dictionary if they cannot figure out the words contextually. Students who read silently may read fluently but not strategically. Words-per-minute does not always indicate a high level of comprehension. Oral fluency needs to be transposed into silent reading fluency.

Periodically, teachers should encourage students to share what they have read. They can increase strategic fluency in several ways, including whole-class or smaller-tiered group discussions, independently completed assignments, guided written questions, and student-and-teacher and peer-to-peer conferencing. They should also increase accessibility to materials such as sticky notes, digital resources, visual dictionaries, and other content-related material on varying levels. These tools encourage students to strategically explore, reflect, and apply critical-thinking skills to what they read and take the next steps to learn more. Students can apply strategic reading principles to analyze mathematics word problems, follow procedures in a science lab, discover music, explore art, interpret historical documents, read a map, download an app, cook a recipe, and more.

Reading is not a race from one period to the next. Teachers must listen to learners read to determine accuracy with prosody, which involves reading's rhythm with pitch, stress, and intonation. Teachers should establish reading speed limits and strategic checkups with more frequent monitoring for students to reflectively engage with the text in meaningful ways.

> *Reading is not a race from one period to the next.*

Reading is meaningless if students cannot read a word or do not understand what they read. It is comparable to visiting a country and not knowing, remembering, or interacting with the sights, sounds, smells, and ambience of the place. Strategic readers play with words, sentences, paragraphs, and chapters in both fiction and nonfiction genres to apply and purposefully make connections to the text.

> *Reading is meaningless if students cannot read a word or do not understand what they read.*

Teachers introduce strategies in Tier 1 and then reinforce them through multiple instructional experiences across diverse genres and applications in Tiers 2 and 3, as warranted. For example, in Tiers 2 and 3, they can increase vocabulary knowledge with more frequent oral discussion and questioning, in written expressions from poems to essays, with group and independent word games, and with continued exposure to a variety of fiction and nonfiction text on students' instructional levels.

Word Decoding

If a student cannot correctly decode words, the teacher can communicate the error through reflection and moving forward steps. For example, if a student reads, "The avatar flew the plane," when the text states, "The aviator flew the plane," then the teacher can use this as a time to point out that although the letters in the words *avatar* and *aviator* are close, the words have two very different meanings. This can lead to a discussion and short lesson on medial vowel pairs and how to use context clues to figure out what a word means. Teachers can do the following to help students decode words.

> *If a student cannot correctly decode words, the teacher can communicate the error through reflection and moving forward steps.*

> ➤ Determine the student's baseline level with an informal reading inventory, and share it with the student. For example, if the student says the word *bit* and the correct word is *bite,* the teacher points out not only the actual pronunciation error but also the type of error, which leads to increased metacognition and practice with *v-e* words.

> ➤ Allow the student to keep track of his or her word decoding success, such as an alphabetical *Words I Now Know* book that the teacher reviews three to four times each week.

> ➤ Administer the same phonics inventory six to eight weeks after guided reading instruction, and share the results with the student so he or she is aware of how reading instruction and effort can yield successful results.

Reading Comprehension

Words are just letters on the page unless students can understand or comprehend what the words mean in context. Teachers can do the following if a student needs help answering reading comprehension questions.

> ➤ Instruct the student on how to preview the reading content and talk about it before he or she actually reads the text. For example, the student notes and comments on headings of an informational article, chapter titles in a novel, and pictures or charts.

> ➤ Provide additional background knowledge with visuals, text, and discussion if a novel occurs in a setting with which the student is unfamiliar. The same holds true for an informational article that contains unfamiliar information.

> ➤ Assist the student to regularly construct and apply *I can* statements. For example, *When I need to answer a comprehension question, I can*:

> • Reread the question and rephrase it in my own words

> • Go back to the text and mark the information (for example, circle the characters or people, underline the key actions, or sort the important facts and details into categories such as *who, what, where, when, why*)

- Discuss the text with an adult or peer

- Think about the question and what kind of information I need to look for

- Say the question and answer aloud to help form and refine thoughts

- Offer repeated and guided practice with minireading comprehension lessons (for example, cause and effect, details, and prediction)

- Teach and relate the comprehension skills to student interests to increase motivation and ease the transfer before the student applies comprehension skills to an unfamiliar knowledge base or content he or she dislikes or that is of little interest

- Follow reading instruction with student and class comprehension celebrations

Students can use the reproducible "Reading Reflection Chart" (page 92) to think about and look back on their reading experiences. This chart assists the teacher in knowing more about his or her students' reading habits and interests. It is also an effective way for students to reflect on their own practices, helping them to discover what next steps are needed to improve reading practice.

Written Expression

Students often struggle to produce effective writing, but practices such as concept mapping, planning, and self-regulation can improve students' writing skills (Flanagan & Bouck, 2015; Reid, Hagaman, & Graham, 2014). Interventions might involve focusing on student behaviors that improve the written product. For example, Reid and colleagues' (2014) study finds that using the self-regulating strategy of POW-TREE helps students with ADHD with essay and story writing. The POW-TREE strategy reminds students to first:

- Plan the essay

- Organize notes

- Write the essay

And then use TREE to focus on the:

- Topic

- Reasons (at least three)

- Explanations for each reason

- Ending

Students who use writing strategies, such as this mnemonic device, produce higher-quality writing because they take more time to plan and have a specific strategy to use. They know more about how to organize the writing. Telling students that they need to improve is fine, but giving them a strategy such as POW-TREE that they can use repeatedly increases long-term success.

Educators should plan more ways to assist students to effectively strategize their writing. If a student needs help with writing, teachers can:

- Share specific writing instruction using models and writing samples that students edit to increase awareness of the writing process rather than emphasize the product

- Offer step-by-step prewriting strategies, such as pictures, content-related word lists, writing prompts, frames with transitional words, open-ended planners, and graphic organizers, to compartmentalize thoughts

➤ Collaborate with gentle writing editors who offer constructive writing reviews (for example, self, peer, teacher, or family member)

➤ Conference with students on a regular basis, pointing out progress and improvements with specific and realistic feedback, such as introduction, word choice, variation of sentence beginnings, details included, sequence of thoughts, and conclusion

➤ Ensure students realize that written expression is a form of communication—to *talk* on paper

➤ Offer empowerment with a choice of topics that honor both the content and student interests to increase confidence and competencies

However, even if a strategy is proven effective, the way the teacher presents the strategy can affect results. The reproducible "Written Expression Chart" (page 93) offers similar strategies from the previous list in a different format. Often, that is the only adaptation a learner requires. Teachers use the first column to identify effective strategies and the second column to reflect on how and when to implement some or all of these strategies.

Learning Environments

Teachers must provide inviting learning environments for students—diverse and structurally inviting to ensure the spaces, resources, preparation, and attitudes complement student levels.

Understanding concepts is important, but examining how and where learning occurs is essential. This includes structuring a classroom within a given space to proactively make available the necessary resources and maximizing each student's contributions, which could be verbal, written, or physical. Eliminating the clutter maximizes student and teacher focus on core instruction and reduces time on extraneous details.

> *Understanding concepts is important, but examining how and where learning occurs is essential.*

If Tier 2 or 3 instruction occurs within the general education setting and not pullout instruction, then the setting should include areas that are free from distractions and that provide teacher and student access to the learning materials (books, writing folders, technology, or mathematics manipulatives). These settings play an important role in student performance (Barrett, Zhang, Moffat, & Kobbacy, 2013). Within those settings, uniqueness, creativity, and curiosity help students flourish and achieve their potential (Gonzales & Young, 2015; Robinson & Aronica, 2015), while classroom designs impact student results (Zhao, 2012).

Classrooms house more than student bodies; they offer opportunities for exploration, personalization, empowerment, and discovery. Differentiation cannot exist if reading materials on different Lexile levels are not available or a multitude of mathematics manipulatives are not accessible. Remediation and acceleration require student-friendly spaces and resources that invite collaborative, personalized, and flexible options.

For example, students with perceptual and learning differences require structures that invite positive attention and places for the cooperative and personalized tiers of instruction and support to happen. These structures might include cooperative learning stations, inviting libraries to explore a variety of genres on diverse reading levels, quiet spaces to reflect, and a variety of exploratory centers to access digital tools and other resources and work individually or with peers. Whether this means offering desks with varying heights, rearranging desks into clusters, or providing sharpened pencils and comfortable beanbag chairs, flexible and meaningful environments should embrace students.

Progress with the core curriculum cannot occur if we continually tell or give students what they need. It is essential that we offer students access to the tools, resources, and knowledge they need within their learning environments to increase learning responsibility with empowerment, monitoring, and feedback.

Teachers can offer resources on strategy tables where students can engage with the content in diverse ways. A strategy table provides opportunities for *just-in-case* scenarios with a UDL approach. What a teacher places on a strategy table depends on what he or she is teaching. If the class is learning multiplication, the teacher might include a hundreds chart to help students practice skip counting or manipulatives so students can create arrays. If students are writing an essay, the teacher might offer writing frames or lists of transitional or sensory words. If the objective in a poetry unit is to teach students about rhyming patterns, the teacher might provide a rhyming dictionary, a variety of poetry selections, and access to sites such as Poetry 180 (www.loc.gov/poetry/180) or RhymeZone (www.rhymezone.com).

Teachers do not need to distribute resources to the whole class; instead, they make resources available for students to choose and access. This allows students to strategically determine what resources they need to further explore concepts and lessons and improve learning. Teachers can then set up ways for students to increase self-regulatory behavior.

Behavior

The classroom environment is composed of abundant emotional, social, and behavioral factors. As noted previously, multitiered instructional practices are best implemented in inviting learning environments. Tier 1 whole-class activities that proactively structure and reinforce the rules are more desirable than punitive ones that at times serve to reinforce negative behaviors. The mentality that lecturing is the best learning style does not do well in modern classrooms or with modern learners. Teachers and students are often challenged with variables such as how to act, what to say, who to collaborate with, and when to assist or request help. Interventions must offer more than examining student behaviors, but also examining teacher response to the behaviors, along with increased student awareness and responsibility for actions and inactions.

Buffum, Mattos, and Weber (2009) note:

> Behavior and academic achievement are inextricably linked. A student's academic success in school is directly related to the student's attention, engagement, and behavior. The higher the expectation for scholarly behaviors and the better the supports for students experiencing difficulties—whether mild, moderate, or severe—the more academic success can be achieved. (p. 111)

As referenced in this quote, proactive measures are valuable to keep behavior and academics on track. For example, a teacher might give a student with autism who prefers consistency a posted schedule and announcements. When a change occurs, such as an assembly, this student would be prepared, and this could possibly prevent inappropriate reactions. A teacher might give a student with test anxiety periodic reviews that occur more often than the day before the exam. Also, the teacher could provide guidelines that outline learning objectives at the onset of a unit of study to help all students know what to expect so they are more prepared to learn.

Every behavior has a reason or a function. Noting antecedents and patterns drives intervention selection, frequency, and intensity. Some students may not verbalize that an assignment is too difficult; instead, their actions or inactions display their frustration. Other students seek attention through their behavior, whether it is positive or negative, having attention-motivated behavior (Rappaport & Minahan, 2012). The following explains behavior interventions at Tiers 1, 2, and 3.

> *Every behavior has a reason or a function.*

Tier 1

The teacher provides the whole class with direct skill instruction on class rules and management, such as:

> ➢ One person speaks at a time.

> ➢ We respect differences.

> ➢ We offer positive comments to peers and adults.

Students can often achieve behavioral strides through literature, so teachers might offer direct skill instruction through fiction and nonfiction examples. Teachers might assign a book from the Lin Oliver and Henry Winkler series *Hank Zipzer* to improve both reading and behavioral skills. Winkler's protagonist, who has dyslexia, is loosely based on his own life. Having students explore what the character does or says can increase awareness of appropriate and inappropriate actions. (The Pinterest board located at www.pinterest.com

/tkarten/disability-books-and-movie-insights -posted-by-toby offers additional books and movies to explore.)

Students can also work in cooperative groups to jigsaw nonfiction articles that focus on role models who faced and effectively dealt with adversity, such as Oprah Winfrey or Albert Einstein. Teachers might empower students to create to-do lists based on behavioral rules observed, read, and shared from classroom practices, peers, and books. Students can use their to-do lists to record class and homework assignments, materials needed, due dates, and more. The purpose of these lists is to increase student reflection, responsibility, organization, and accountability.

For example, a seventh grader I worked with needed help to address his impulsiveness and frequent disregard for classroom rules. A staff team effort of communications, observations, and work performance revealed progress from September through December, but then team members refined our goals to modify the plan. We met again in January as a collaborative team after I observed his behaviors in several classes. We formulated a goal for this student so he could be the proprietor of his strategies and outlined specific skills he needed to hone. We designed a plan for a gradual release of responsibility to the student for acquiring steady academic and behavioral skill achievements for the remainder of the school year. We worked on this list with him, as a group, throughout the year.

> ➢ Independence (fewer prompts for task completion)

> ➢ Transitions (within classes and moving to next classes)

> ➢ Self-help (self-monitor; decrease nail biting)

➤ Focus (increase attention)

➤ Cooperative group work (take turns; listen)

➤ Internalization (*own it!*)

Tier 2

Students who still display inappropriate behaviors require additional guidance with schedule or program modifications that range from extra time on a test, to additional physical exercise and more flexible assignments. Teachers can provide incremental reinforcement, increased verbal feedback, teacher conferencing, and calming strategies that increase self-regulation three times each week for forty- to forty-five-minute periods to increase awareness and replace unsuitable actions with more productive ones. Teachers should also collaborate with other school staff and family. For example, a school psychologist, guidance counselor, special education teacher, or paraprofessional can assist with observation and student conferencing.

Tier 3

Some students require more intensive interventions. They might be withdrawn or depressed, defiant, overly anxious, and display interrupting behaviors. These students require constructive actions that involve a behavioral interventionist, school psychologist, guidance counselor, and other related school staff assisting and consulting them daily to increase awareness of how students should act and behave toward themselves and others. In addition, families should be on board with consistent strategies reinforced in all environments. Educators should communicate with families about what goes on in school regarding rules and structures so there is consistency, reinforcement, and the additional practice and application of skills in all settings.

Assistance with behavioral, social, and emotional factors requires teachers to structure and review the data with progress monitoring that reinforces but does not judge or belittle. Students need to know that they are liked but that their behavior needs to be revisited. As with the building of the Roman Empire, nothing happens in a day; however, evolutionary and proactive measures can catapult positive results.

Assessment Data

RTI and differentiation cannot occur without assessment data because they are the foundation that meaningfully drives instruction. Assessments refine and improve both teaching practices and student learning and performance (Carnegie Mellon University, n.d.). Screening, diagnostic, formative progress monitoring, benchmark progress monitoring, and summative outcome assessments are all types of data (Wixson & Valencia, 2011). The National Center on Response to Intervention (n.d.) outlines three types of assessment: (1) diagnostic, (2) formative, and (3) summative, which help teachers evaluate student levels.

Diagnostic assessments determine student levels to identify both strengths and weaknesses. Teachers usually give these tests before instruction so they can offer responsive enrichment and remediation (National Center on Response to Intervention, n.d.). Examples of diagnostic assessments include Qualitative Reading Inventory, Group Reading Assessment and Diagnostic Evaluation, and KeyMath-3.

Formative assessments can consist of curriculum-based measurements or informal quizzes or observations. Formal formative assessment indexes a student's mastery of increasing successes with lesson objectives and skills, or it can note the overall annual growth, known as general outcome measures (National Center on Response to

Intervention, n.d.). Teachers collect formative data during instruction, which leads to instructional changes in response to learners' social, emotional, and behavioral needs. Formative data include observation, work samples, teacher-made tests, written and oral quizzes, open-ended questions, student conferencing, homework, and more. Formative assessments help to inform instruction. Formal examples of formative assessments include Dynamic Indicators of Basic Early Literacy Skills (DIBELS) and AIMSweb System Review.

Curriculum-based measurement, a type of formative assessment, determines whether a student needs assistance to acquire a skill or if he or she has fluency in a given subject or with a behavioral expectation to achieve mastery (Malouf, Reisener, Gadke, Wimbish, & Frankel, 2014). First, teachers must establish proficiency baseline levels, which are the starting points of what students know, to drive student goals and interventions to measure progress. Then, at set times, such as after a four- to six-week instructional period, they compare student progress to grade levels or benchmarks to note improvements or lack of response or progress to the interventions.

Curriculum-based measurement provides multileveled progress monitoring to note student learning growth at set and frequent time intervals (for example, biweekly, weekly, or monthly). Teachers can graph change over time to offer accurate student information that drives the selection of interventions. Curriculum-based measurement is often used to gauge the progress of students with IEPs to strengthen instructional planning and student achievement (Stecker, n.d.). Curriculum-based measurement leads students on paths to achieve mastery. Improvements reveal important information on whether the instructional program appropriately targets whole-class,

small-group, and individual levels of both grade-level and struggling students.

Summative assessments generally occur after a longer period of instructional time, such as end-of-unit chapter tests, and may involve standardized tests to determine what students have learned. These kinds of assessments can include end-of-course mathematics or history tests, STAAR, or an SAT. Screening is essential for both academic and behavioral skills.

Teachers must implement reliable and valid assessments to determine academic levels that include, but are not limited to, reading, written expression, spelling, and mathematics. These curriculum measurements note areas such as words read correctly per minute, computation skills, critical-thinking applications, and effective writing skills, such as creating well-structured sentences.

Tests such as AIMSweb, STAAR, DIBELS, and the Development Reading Assessment indicate baseline levels. EasyCBM (https://app.easycbm .com) offers tools and resources to measure K–8 reading and mathematics levels, including phoneme segmentation to word passage reading and mathematics skills with numbers and operations, ratios, geometry, and algebra. The Research Institute on Progress Monitoring (www .progressmonitoring.org) evaluates learner progress and teacher instruction within the general education curriculum.

The ultimate goal of curriculum-based measurement is for teachers to analyze data to decide on appropriate instruction. Teachers note achievement levels over time on set goals. Education assessment professor Robert Stake states the difference between formative and summative assessment in simple terms, "When the cook tastes the soup, that's formative. When the guests taste the soup, that's summative" (as cited in Scriven, 1991, p. 169).

In closing, school staff are the ones who not only buy the ingredients for the soup, but also regulate the temperature to prepare the soup, and then thoughtfully and skillfully serve the meal to their diverse guests, known as students.

Multiple Curriculum Entry Points

Successfully navigating best practices means that there are "multiple ports" to enter the curriculum. Teaching a concept multiple ways respects students' diverse learning styles; teachers will engage students that prefer visuals, sound, movement, or some other method that acknowledges learner interests and multiple intelligences. The curriculum (what is taught), instruction (how it is taught), and assessment (how to measure what is taught) should be as varied as students; and instruction and intervention should be responsive to student diversity.

Cross-curricular instruction integrates knowledge across subject areas, rather than teaching each discipline in isolation. Students are able to transfer skills and knowledge in order to understand concepts more fully (Hickman & Kiss, 2010). As a best practice, cross-curricular instruction offers multiple entry points to the curriculum with links to other subjects. Teachers can activate and reinforce prior knowledge through multiple lessons and broader lenses, rather than presenting information in an isolated lesson through one type of engagement that may not coincide with a student's learning preferences. The following lesson plans are good examples of best practices in RTI.

> *Cross-curricular instruction integrates knowledge across subject areas, rather than teaching each discipline in isolation.*

MTSS Lesson Connections

The big idea is that cross-curricular lessons increase student engagement. Diverse lesson engagements value the equally diverse classroom, not singling out students for their differences. Figures 4.2–4.9 (pages 79–83) feature elementary, middle school, and high school lessons that connect both the curriculum and student interests to present interdisciplinary, cross-curricular units. (Visit **go.SolutionTree.com/RTI** to access more free reproducible lesson examples.)

These lessons model various teaching methods for multiple subjects and grade levels. For example, the fifth-grade lesson has students explore the 1987 novel *Hatchet* by Gary Paulsen, with art, music, theater, and technology. Teachers can use the reproducible "Lesson-Planning Template: Lessons Across the Disciplines" (page 94) to plan lessons in any discipline.

During the lesson, the teacher reads the novel's first three chapters aloud, as students listen and record Paulsen's sensory elements in a sensory planner, as shown in figure 4.3. He or she outlines the vivid words in the book that describe the action in the planner.

Students write a book report after completing the planner. Teachers should provide a writing frame similar to that shown in figure 4.4 (page 80) for students to organize their thoughts. They can also use the sensory planner as a model.

Scenario: A fifth-grade class includes students at lower reading and writing levels. One student with cerebral palsy has fine motor issues and less physical stamina.	
Learning Goal	Students practice and increase reading comprehension skills with a novel study.
Resources	Each student needs a copy of the book *Hatchet* by Gary Paulsen (1987), writing planners, and maps of the United States and Canada.
Cross-Curricular Connections	**Reading, writing, and emotional:** Students investigate themes of resiliency and fortitude in reference to the challenges that Brian faces and compare this to a personal experience of someone they know who also faced a difficult situation. This should lead to discussion and critical thinking through "what if" scenarios. **Social studies and mathematics:** Students plot Brian's journey on a map and calculate the distance and time he traveled in the plane. They can compare this to other transportation options Brian could have selected, such as a car or train. Students can work in cooperative groups to create comparative graphs. **Science:** Students investigate the following concepts. • Weather patterns and seasons in the United States versus Canada • Signs of a heart attack • How transformers work **Art, music, theater, and technology:** The teacher provides learning centers where students work in groups of three to five to complete one of six assignments in the Show What You Know chart (figure 4.5), which includes a choice of creating a PowerPoint, a test, skit, poem, travel brochure, or song.
Multitiered System of Supports	**Tier 1:** All students access digital tools. The teacher activates the accessibility feature with word prediction for the student with cerebral palsy. The teacher provides instruction for the student in Tier 1, but allows him to record his answers. The teacher gives this student extra time with more frequent breaks if his stamina is lower. **Tier 2:** This targeted group reads different leveled articles from Newsela (https://newsela.com/text-sets/9832/books--hatchet-paulsen) to learn more about *Hatchet*'s themes, such as man versus nature and initiation into adulthood. The instructional assistant offers reading guidance and monitors student progress under teacher direction each day. **Tier 3:** These students read an adapted graphic novel version of *Hatchet*. The general education teacher provides them with simplified writing planners and transitional lists, while the co-teacher (who is present during this period) provides increased feedback and direct reading skill instruction four times each week for fifty-minute periods.

Figure 4.2: Grade 5 literacy lesson on *Hatchet*.

Hear	See	Smell	Touch	Taste
hum of small plane	plane flew straight	skunk sprayed Brian	sat frozen	tart blueberries
voice got fainter	looked for a meadow		legs felt like lead	
insects buzzing	L-shaped lake		felt weeds on the bank	

Figure 4.3: Sample sensory planner for *Hatchet*.

Use the following writing frame to organize your thoughts.

First Paragraph (Introduction)

The story's action begins with thirteen-year-old Brian Robeson, who _____. He left for Canada because _____. Unexpectedly, _____. The most interesting thing about the beginning of the story is that _____.

Second Paragraph (Sensory Details From Chart)

The author uses many descriptions of sights, sounds, smells, and tastes when _____. Some include _____ and _____. _____ sounds like _____, and _____ looks like _____. The most exciting part is when _____ and _____.

Third Paragraph (Conclusion)

Overall, *Hatchet* is about _____. It can best be described as _____, _____, and _____. The hatchet symbolizes _____. To sum up, I think *Hatchet* _____.

Figure 4.4: Sample writing frame for *Hatchet*.

(Visit **go.SolutionTree.com/RTI** to download a free reproducible blank sensory planner and writing frame.)

Students can use figure 4.5 to brainstorm ways to present to the class what they learned from reading *Hatchet*.

The reproducible "Curriculum Dice Game" (page 95) offers a blank template teachers can use to play this game in their classrooms in any discipline.

Learner Outcomes

When there is a disconnect between the lesson objectives and positive student outcomes, teachers must re-examine their instructional practices and lesson plans to ensure they are providing curriculum entry points that are responsive to learner levels and evidenced progress. Learner outcomes hinge on the multitiered system of supports based on student competencies achieved in response to evidence-based interventions. Performance data and monitoring learning rates through a multitiered system of supports guide instructional decisions to reach students with diverse backgrounds, learning styles, and levels of skill attainment (Gamm et al., 2012).

Academic and behavioral decisions should be data based. Differentiated instruction and universal design for learning acknowledge the merits of offering students multiple types of access to the concepts. Teachers can accomplish this with varying engagements, representations, actions, and expressions. Examining learner outcomes determines more than a pass-or-fail outcome; it helps determine which discrete step or part of a concept requires additional or alternate engagement and representation. When teachers examine outcomes on a personal basis, they not only acknowledge the concept, but most important, value the student.

> *Academic and behavioral decisions should be data based.*

Learner outcomes are connected with instructional decisions and the environment where teachers deliver instruction. A competency-based, personalized approach that includes instruction and learning goals tailored to each student is essential for learners to move from passive recipient to active learning partner (Rickabaugh, 2015).

Hatchet: Show What You Know Create or design a . . .		
☐ PowerPoint of at least eight slides with six sequential events that Brian experienced	☐ Poem about survival skills (model the format of a poem that you like)	☐ Travel brochure about the Canadian wilderness, including pictures and captions
☐ Skit about the events, including three different scenes	☐ Test about the story's events, varying your question types and including an answer key	☐ Song about Brian's journey, including events from the beginning to the end and using your sensory planner

Figure 4.5: Presentation brainstorming chart for Hatchet.

Scenario: A seventh-grade class has five students with lower reading levels. Several students have difficulties encoding multisyllabic words.	
Learning Goal	Students identify the theme, mood, and tone of a poem.
Resources	Each student needs a copy of the short story "The Tell-Tale Heart" by Edgar Allan Poe (1843), science texts, graphic and paperback novels, circulatory system diagrams, and digital tools.
Cross-Curricular Connections	With a partner, students read Edgar Allan Poe's (1843) short story, "The Tell-Tale Heart." The teacher gives students story maps to complete and then discusses student-generated oral and written questions about the poem's theme and mood. **Science and art:** Students create a model of the heart with clay or paper as the medium. **Physical education and mathematics:** Students take their pulse by calculating their heart rate with their wrist and neck. They calculate their target heart-rate zone using the HealthCheck Systems website (www.healthchecksystems.com/heart.asp). Students then compare their heart rate after engaging in physical exercise with peers, such as a basketball game, capture the flag, or dodgeball.
Social and Emotional Connections	Students discuss and analyze this quote from Antoine de Saint-Exupéry's (1943) The Little Prince, "And now here is my secret, a very simple secret: It is only with the heart that one can see rightly; what is essential is invisible to the eye."
Multitiered System of Supports	**Tier 1:** The teacher provides instruction for all students on the poem's theme, mood, and tone with instructional videos and ties to the concepts. **Tier 2:** The teacher offers an audiobook and graphic novel adaptation of the poem as instruction for a smaller group of students. Students can review vocabulary and concepts at the KidsHealth website (http://kidshealth.org/en/kids/heart.html) with the text-to-speech tools activated. Students then practice additional comprehension skills three times each week with a co-teacher offering more modeling, guidance, and feedback. **Tier 3:** Instead of creating a model of the heart, students label the parts of the circulatory system on printed circulatory system diagrams with word boxes provided (for example, a-or-ta, cap-il-lar-ies, veins, blood ves-sels). The school reading interventionist provides these students with direct skill instruction on how to encode multisyllabic words through an Orton-Gillingham approach five times each week. Orton-Gillingham is a research-based reading approach that teaches students who struggle with reading the explicit connections between letters and sounds through multisensory, structured instruction (Academy of Orton-Gillingham Practitioners and Educators, 2012; Rosen, 2016).

Figure 4.6: Grade 7 interdisciplinary lesson.

Scenario: A tenth-grade history class is starting a unit on immigration. The students have varying attention spans and motivations to learn. The immigration unit begins with invited guests who share their immigrant experiences (teachers' and students' relatives).	
Learning Goal	Students extract information from primary and secondary sources and communicate findings in cooperative teams.
Resources	Students need online and hands-on sources, including primary and secondary documents with multiple materials for students to gain access to immigration information. Primary sources offer original documents, historical artifacts, and other specific cultural material, while secondary sources include articles, books, and information from people who did not experience the events firsthand. Class visitors relating their actual experiences are considered a primary source. The multitude of sources increases student perspectives and knowledge based on actual events and research.
	Students and teachers also need the following from the Library of Congress primary-source set.
	• "Immigrants and Immigration: Answering the Tough Questions" (American Federation of State, County, and Municipal Employees, n.d.): http://bit.ly/2ffwhDo
	• "U.S. Immigration Before 1965" (History, n.d.b): www.history.com/topics/u-s-immigration-before-1965
	• "Immigration: Challenges for New Americans" (Library of Congress, n.d.a): www.loc.gov/teachers /classroommaterials/primarysourcesets/immigration
	• "Spring 2010 Teaching With Primary Sources Quarterly Learning Activity: Secondary Level— Understanding Immigration Through Popular Culture" (Library of Congress, 2010): http://bit.ly/2eQVY9d
	• "Largest U.S. Immigrant Groups Over Time, 1960–Present" (Migration Policy Institute, 2014): www.migrationpolicy.org/programs/data-hub/charts/largest-immigrant-groups-over-time
	• "For Educators: Lesson Plan Index—Immigration Policy, Past and Present" (PBS: Independent Lens, 2015): http://to.pbs.org/2flTgqz
	• "Immigration Myths" (Teaching Tolerance, n.d.): www.tolerance.org/lesson/immigration-myths
Cross-Curricular Connections	The subjects in this lesson use reading, writing, research, music, history, and technology. Students cooperatively complete projects on immigrant groups who entered the United States during the respective time periods. Students learn reading, writing, research, music, history, technology, and group work skills and objectives during this lesson.
Multitiered System of Supports	**Tier 1:** The teacher instructs the whole class on what an immigrant is and the different groups that entered the United States. In this project-based learning activity, students then research immigrant groups entering the United States. They jigsaw three different time periods for a specific group or country, and then share findings in each team presentation.
	• Early U.S. history (1700s–mid-1800s)
	• Ellis Island (1892–1954)
	• 1954–present
	Each team presents findings on its selected immigrant group to the rest of the class. Jigsawing the immigrant groups allows students to increase their knowledge about various immigrant groups, gain behavioral work skills as they divide responsibilities with peers, learn how to conduct research, and gain more practice on how to deliver effective presentations.
	Tier 2: A paraprofessional under the direction of a special education teacher provides additional small-group instruction and monitoring for two students who have IEPs and lower reading and behavioral levels. The paraprofessional helps the two students conduct research, access documents, create presentations, and share information with Word and PowerPoint features on their digital devices. Increased staff regulation and feedback increase their focus and time on task since even though there are hyperlinked sites, these students cannot independently navigate online. The paraprofessional explains more difficult vocabulary in the primary documents through small-group activities, such as pantomiming the vocabulary, using accompanying visuals, and accessing digital flash cards to grasp the big ideas on immigrants.
	Tier 3: One student requires the daily assistance and consultation of a behavioral interventionist. The teacher offers a cooperative immigration dice game for review (see figure 4.9). This dice game format encourages the student to become more engaged. The idea is to roll the dice and focus on the descriptor by each number. Students can also work with virtual dice at Curriculumbits.com (2007; http://bit.ly/2bgaOYT). They use it to input a variety of content that students can complete independently or in small groups across the disciplines.

Figure 4.7: Grade 10 immigration informational article lesson.

Points	Requirements
15 points	Reason immigrant group left its country
15 points	Contributions to U.S. culture: art, music, dance, science, mathematics, books, technology, politics
15 points	Discrimination experienced, including specific legislation if applicable
15 points	Review of primary documents related to one of the immigrant groups
20 points	Class presentation including digital media (for example, skit, speech, debate)
10 points	Contribution to annotated class Immigration Time Line (www.readwritethink.org/classroom-resources/student-interactives/timeline-30007.html; www.knowledgequestmaps.com/TimelineBuilder.html)
10 points	Sources cited in APA format, posted on class Edmodo (www.edmodo.com) page

Figure 4.8: Immigration project requirements.

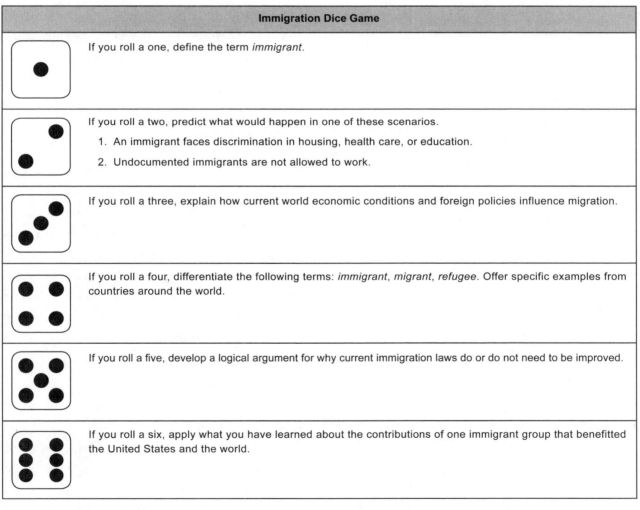

Immigration Dice Game
If you roll a one, define the term *immigrant*.
If you roll a two, predict what would happen in one of these scenarios. 1. An immigrant faces discrimination in housing, health care, or education. 2. Undocumented immigrants are not allowed to work.
If you roll a three, explain how current world economic conditions and foreign policies influence migration.
If you roll a four, differentiate the following terms: *immigrant*, *migrant*, *refugee*. Offer specific examples from countries around the world.
If you roll a five, develop a logical argument for why current immigration laws do or do not need to be improved.
If you roll a six, apply what you have learned about the contributions of one immigrant group that benefitted the United States and the world.

Source: ©Toby Karten. Used with permission.

Figure 4.9: Immigration dice game.

Learner outcomes must be student centered. This includes inviting students to establish a sense of purpose.

If students are not successful, teachers might consider inviting colleagues, students, and families to examine how to improve the learning outcomes. Together, they can discuss the following considerations to raise learner outcomes and achieve greater student success.

➤ Teacher considerations:

- How can I teach this concept differently?

- Which part of the concept requires additional explanation?

- Can I repeat the concept or skill as the curriculum continues?

- Do I shift blame onto students and their parents when students don't learn, or do I reflect on the intensity and frequency of practice?

➤ Student considerations:

- Do I know what outcomes I need to achieve?

- Did I try my best?

- What questions do I have, and did I ask them?

- Do I blame the teacher for not teaching me the material when I don't learn?

➤ Family considerations:

- How can we collaborate to support learning at home?

- Do we collaborate with the school and staff or blame them when our child doesn't learn?

- Is everyone on the same team, having the same definition of the learning outcomes, holding the belief that responsibility is shared by educators, families, and students?

This chapter's lessons offer a multitiered system of supports, cross-curricular connections, and social and emotional connections. The reproducible "Lesson-Planning Template: Lessons Across the Disciplines" (page 94) provides a template teachers can use to include student personalization and family collaboration as an integral part of the multitiered system of supports. As teachers plan their lessons, they must proactively engage multitiered supports and diverse engagements, including personalization with social, emotional, and behavioral connections.

Conclusion

Best practices mean that cross-curricular lessons connect the concepts and skills to diverse subjects and students. When planning lessons, teachers must embrace and factor in student diversity with attention to cognition, behavior, communication, and culture. Learning should occur in student- and teacher-friendly formats, and teachers should offer accommodations and modifications within tiered instruction based on student response to the lesson's complexity, their prior skill sets, and other disciplines.

Best practices recognize that classrooms house more than student bodies; they offer opportunities for exploration, personalization, empowerment, and discovery. To be effective, tiered instruction includes core instruction for the whole class and then additional tiers, as needed, for struggling learners as teachers diversify the curriculum (what is taught), instruction (how it is taught), and assessment (how to measure what is taught).

Response to student variability occurs with planned learning maps, individualization, and respect for learner growth, with fidelity to evidence-based practices. A collaborative, problem-solving approach replaces student and school staff frustration with quality instruction that infuses academic and behavioral interventions and supports. With proactive approaches, teachers can more easily navigate the challenges students present with solutions for transforming academic and behavioral deficits into school and lifelong success.

Parts of a Book

Name: _____	
Directions: Fill in information about your book.	
Title	
Author	
Year Written	
Illustrator	
Front Cover	
Back Cover	
Summary (three to five sentences)	
Favorite Part or Chapter (three to five sentences)	
Picture With a Caption	
Table of Contents	
Index	

Syllable Types

Name: _____

Directions: Find at least five words with these syllables. If the word has more than one syllable, highlight or underline the syllable type.

Closed	Vowel-Consonant-e	Open Syllables	Vowel Teams	r-Controlled	Consonant-le
bat, fig, pup	smile, hope, love	no, he, hi	fair, meat, play	more, far, first, <u>pur</u>ple	han<u>dle</u>, an<u>gle</u>, pur<u>ple</u>

Words and Questions Chart

Name: _____

Directions: Review the text and respond to these prompts.

Word Exploration	Assignment
Affixes and Roots	List four words in the passage that have affixes. 1. _____ 2. _____ 3. _____ 4. _____
Document-Based Vocabulary	Select four vocabulary words to compose a text-related sentence. 1. _____ 2. _____ 3. _____ 4. _____ Sentence: _____ _____ _____
Picture Response	Draw a picture of a word you learned.
Syllables	List four words that have three or more syllables. 1. _____ 2. _____ 3. _____ 4. _____
Classification	Select five words to sort into the following categories: nouns, verbs, adjectives, and adverbs. <table><tr><td>Nouns</td><td>Verbs</td><td>Adjectives</td><td>Adverbs</td></tr><tr><td></td><td></td><td></td><td></td></tr><tr><td></td><td></td><td></td><td></td></tr><tr><td></td><td></td><td></td><td></td></tr></table>
Compare and Contrast	Think about what you just read and compare it to another point of view on the same topic. Record answers in a Venn diagram.

People, Places, and Things Chart

Name: _____

Directions: Identify the important people (characters), places, and things you read about in the novel, passage, article, or text.

People	Places	Things

Write a paragraph describing the important people, places, and things you read about. Use three words from each column.	Use this space to write your paragraph.

Nine words used:

Record of Mathematics Skills, Concepts, and Engagements

Name: _____

Directions: Identify student levels with the computations, concepts, and applications to begin, continue, and fine-tune mathematical skills. Note learner engagements, representations, and applications. Check off appropriate descriptors to document your practices.

Beginning Mathematics Skills	Continuing Mathematics Skills	Fine-Tuning Mathematics Skills
☐ Concrete representations	☐ Challenge	☐ Discrete-task analysis
☐ Visual representations	☐ Effective questioning	☐ Formal mathematics assessment
☐ Abstract representations	☐ Thinking skills	☐ Informal mathematics assessment
☐ Ongoing computational drills	☐ Real-life applications	
☐ Compact skills	☐ Multiple representations	☐ Guide
☐ Specific feedback	☐ Numerical representation	☐ Monitor
☐ Number sense	☐ Graphical representation	☐ Reinforce
☐ Whole numbers	☐ Symbolic representation	☐ Tutorials
☐ Addition	☐ Verbal representation	☐ Daily drills
☐ Subtraction	☐ Pictorial representation	☐ Independent practice
☐ Multiplication	☐ Mathematics learning centers	☐ Scaffolding
☐ Division	☐ Mathematics skits	☐ Think-alouds
☐ Estimation	☐ High expectations	☐ Extra time
☐ Mental computation	☐ Mathematics games	☐ Different pacing
☐ Money	☐ Mathematics "shout-outs" that celebrate the progress	☐ Frequent feedback
☐ Time	☐ Other: _____	☐ Praise for partial mastery
☐ Measurement		☐ Peer support
☐ Geometry		☐ Increased metacognition
☐ Fractions		☐ Real-life applications
☐ Decimals		☐ Other: _____
☐ Percentages		
☐ Ratios		
☐ Proportions		
☐ Patterns and relationships		
☐ Algebra		
☐ Probability		
☐ Statistics		
☐ Real-life applications		
☐ Other: _____		

Record of Student Participation

Students	Dates	Multitiered Accommodations or Modifications	With Accommodations	With Modifications	Parallel, Related Assignment, or Task	Additional Comments or Supports: Accommodations, Modifications, and Proficiency Levels
		☐ Full participation ☐ Partial participation				
		☐ Full participation ☐ Partial participation				
		☐ Full participation ☐ Partial participation				

Reading Reflection Chart

Name: _____

Directions: Complete the chart to reflect on your reading experience.

I am a skilled reader, because I:

- ☐ Preview the text
- ☐ Talk about what I read
- ☐ Reread the text
- ☐ Think about what I read
- ☐ Ask questions
- ☐ Read for enjoyment
- ☐ Read to learn
- ☐ Read to write
- ☐ Read a variety of books and genres
- ☐ Research more

My Reading Comments

Written Expression Chart

If a student needs help with written expression, offer the following strategies.

Metacognitive Strategies	Comments and Dates
Offer guided step-by-step instruction.	
Emphasize the process, not the product.	
Provide models.	
Provide writing rubrics.	
Give interim feedback.	
Scaffold as needed using pictures, content-related word lists, writing prompts, frames with transitional words, open-ended planners, and graphic organizers, to compartmentalize thoughts.	
Collaborate with gentle writing editors who offer constructive writing reviews (for example, self, peer, teacher, family).	
Conference with students on a regular basis, pointing out progress and improvements with specific and realistic feedback (for example, introduction, word choice, variation of sentence beginnings, details included, sequence of thoughts, conclusion).	
Empower students with a choice of topics that honor both the content and student interests to increase writing competency and confidence.	
Ensure students realize that written expression is a form of communication, to talk on paper and then edit those expressions.	

Lesson-Planning Template: Lessons Across the Disciplines

Class Background (provide information about the class):	
Learning Goal	Students will (state the learning goal):
Resources	Students will need (list the resources):
Cross-Curricular Connections	(List the subjects—reading, language, history, mathematics, science, physical education, music, art, theater, dance, and so on—being studied.)
Multitiered System of Supports	The following occurs at Tiers 1, 2, and 3 (state what occurs at each tier). • **Tier 1:** • **Tier 2:** • **Tier 3:**
Social-Emotional-Behavioral Connections	
Student Personalization	
Family Collaboration	

Curriculum Dice Game

	_____ **Dice Game**
⚀	If you roll a one, define:
⚁	If you roll a two, predict what would happen in one of these scenarios: 1. _____ _____ 2. _____ _____
⚂	If you roll a three, explain:
⚃	If you roll a four, differentiate the following terms:
⚄	If you roll a five, develop a logical argument for:
⚅	If you roll a six, apply what you have learned about:

CHAPTER **5**

OFFERING ACADEMIC AND BEHAVIORAL SUPPORT

In schools and classrooms, decisions are made collaboratively. Decisions, which teachers, students, and families collaboratively formulate, are based on individual learners' academic and behavioral levels. Teachers should never view students as the problem. Instead, they should view academic and behavioral problems as challenges, and then identify and address these challenges with the appropriate interventions. Supportive academic and behavioral interventions combine to raise student achievement.

> *Teachers should never view students as the problem.*

This chapter offers strategies that include positive behavior interventions that emphasize increased monitoring to provide realistic, student-centered data to inform instruction and multiple interventions. Multiple interventions acknowledge that each student has diverse skill sets with a variety of likes, dislikes, triggers, and motivations. Therefore, the verbal praise that works for one student may not work for another. A student may respond more positively to feedback from an online site or app that demonstrates and reinforces behavioral, social, and emotional skills with digital tools, such as a virtual community of avatars who interact with one another, or perhaps a low-tech smile would be just as effective. Furthermore, behavioral decisions often impact academics.

The chapter also offers lessons with student-specific, multitiered supports that teachers can use to respond to student differences. The lessons are applicable to students with behavioral and academic issues as well as those without them. Figure 5.1 (page 98) illustrates the structure of this chapter.

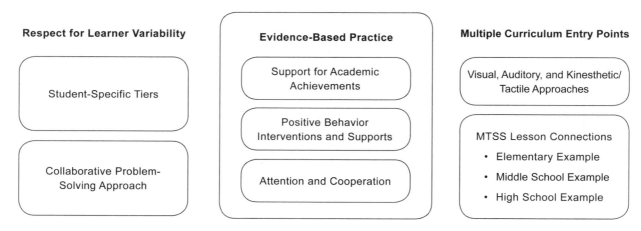

Figure 5.1: Plan for offering academic and behavioral support.

Respect for Learner Variability

Respecting learner variability requires instruction that values structure, flexibility, and individuality. When we take a trip, we usually have an itinerary planned. However, delays for road construction or different weather conditions sometimes change our original plan. Although we structured the trip in one way, we require flexibility to adapt and create a new course. The same holds true for our classroom lessons. The lessons are the road map, but individual students *drive the implementation.*

Research-based instructional strategies should accompany all tiers of intervention with flexible and responsive supports, including consistency, guided practice, modeling, multiple means of VAKT elements, and specific and timely feedback. Whether teachers provide whole-class, small-group, or individualized instruction, they need to respect learner variability. Students should have the opportunity to learn in a variety of ways that honor their diverse learning levels and skill sets. Structure is required, but so is flexibility and individualization.

Student-Specific Tiers

Although learning is often subject specific, the tiers are student specific, because teachers and collaborative teams identify the specific students who need additional help beyond the core instruction. Research-based core strategies for literacy, mathematics, cross-curricular academics, and behavioral, social, and emotional outcomes acknowledge, value, and appropriately present the concepts in tiers to students who require differentiation. Tier 2 and Tier 3 interventions have increasing student specificity. Beginning with Tier 2 instruction, teachers select interventions that help improve the areas where students need support. They apply intensive instructional practices and schedule frequent progress monitoring, which teachers review collaboratively with colleagues.

Tier 3 offers more intensive instruction for small groups and individual students who require additional intervention. The instruction that these students receive within Tier 2 is just not enough. They might require alternate formats and time to learn prerequisite background knowledge that they lack, such as oral fluency, comprehension skills, and mathematical, computational, or conceptual skills.

Collaborative Problem-Solving Approach

Teachers can accomplish screening, planning, monitoring, instructing, assessing students' levels, and determining whether students are responding to interventions with a collaborative team approach. Collaborative problem solving involves classroom general and education staff, administrators, related service providers, families, and students, as appropriate. The team reviews data and reflectively problem solves to determine the effectiveness of instruction and interventions.

According to Thomas R. Hoerr (2016), problem solving also involves nonscholastic intelligences, which go beyond the reading, language, and mathematics acumens that allow students to express their knowledge. This includes honoring cultural and linguistic differences and other intelligences, such as Gardner's (1995) theory of multiple intelligences and Sternberg's (2014) triarchic theory. For example, teachers might allow students to demonstrate their learning through an art collage, a song, or a dance. Hoerr (2016) writes that the key is to turn or spin learner challenges into growth.

Additionally, teachers can combine Hoerr's (2016) outlook with George Pólya's (1957) four-step problem-solving approach.

1. Teachers identify each student's level of performance. They use observation, screening, data collection, and review to accomplish this.

2. Teachers match identified student needs to intervention plans that include multitiered supports delivered to the whole class, small groups, and individuals. Applying Pólya's steps requires infusing subgoals for the academic and behavioral patterns as warranted. To do this, teachers dissect academic and behavioral objectives into their smaller components. The idea is that a student can often complete some parts of the academic requirements, but not others. So, the collaborative team identifies which parts require more intervention with instruction geared to these specific parts.

3. Teachers carry out the intervention plan—implementing the steps and recording and monitoring progress.

4. Teachers collaborate to analyze students' responses to multitiered interventions to reflect on the intervention plan.

In order to move forward, educators must absorb and comprehend prior *classroom expository*. Simply stated, what happens before helps determine where students go next. Communications from past and current teachers, related service providers, and families shed insights that a teacher then factors into an RTI problem-solving approach. Students' responses to the interventions compose and reveal the expository. Teachers then use information that students reveal in their behaviors and academic progress, or lack of progress, to responsively tweak lessons. They must reflect to move forward. Reviewing the learning terrain traveled yields much mileage.

> *Educators must absorb and comprehend prior* classroom expository.

Just as navigators control and orient the movement of a craft or vehicle from one place to another, educators are responsible for learners' mobility from one accomplishment to the next.

Using a different analogy, Sandra Cisneros's (n.d.) short story *Eleven* compares growing up to the layers of an onion or the rings of a tree. One year is contained and influenced by the one before. Just like an ant colony is stronger than an individual ant or a human being is composed of cells that make up his or her tissues, organs, and systems, RTI is a sum of its parts, divided into multiple tiers that are collaboratively established, reviewed, and interrelated from one lesson to the next as the grades progress.

Evidence-Based Practice

Learning is divided into components that involve teachers and support staff, students, and evidence-based practice. How learning progresses depends on whether staff construct a plan that is based on the facts, implement it with fidelity, and then reflect on that plan to determine its validity and whether tweaking is required. The one non-negotiable is that a teacher has high expectations for *all* his or her students. Evidence-based practice must provide a variety of engagements and supports that address students' academic and behavioral needs.

Support for Academic Achievements

Teachers can support students' academic achievements through various pathways, including, for example, direct skill instruction, guided explicit practice, parallel lessons, learning stations or centers, sponge activities, and student conferencing).

➤ Direct instruction includes lectures, verbal directions, and demonstrations.

➤ Guided explicit practice includes modeling and monitoring.

➤ Parallel lessons include, but are not limited to, having students of mixed skill levels work in two groups on the same or similar concepts, with different parts of the lesson and the appropriate scaffolding and resources.

➤ Learning stations or centers offer ongoing classroom projects, instructional resources, and activities set up in specific classroom locations that allow students to manipulate and explore the concepts with opportunities for practice, remediation, and enrichment.

➤ Sponge activities include activities for learners to expand and absorb the knowledge.

➤ Student conferencing allows conversations about academic as well as social and behavioral issues that invite increased metacognition in a nonthreatening way to clarify students' questions or concerns about academic concepts and classroom routines and expectations.

These multiple interventions provide instructional delivery within a framework that connects to and ignites students to learn. This includes evidence-based interventions that teachers deliver with integrity and fidelity to students' levels to support high expectations for academic achievement.

Positive Behavior Interventions and Supports

Educators across the United States have frequently shared with me that their biggest challenge is student behavior. They have an excellent command of their subject area, but often student behavior makes the instructional road a complicated one to navigate. Establishing appropriate classroom behavior precedes instruction, since students who display inappropriate behaviors are learning less and also can set other students off course.

A schoolwide behavior management program, known as Positive Behavioral Interventions and Supports (PBIS), helps teachers who are challenged in the area of classroom management (Reinke, Herman, & Stormont, 2013). Teachers should deliver PBIS on a continuum to assist students with emotional, social, and behavioral needs (Benner, Kutash, Nelson, & Fisher, 2013). Ideally, these needs should not get in the way of learning, but they often do. Students might display different behaviors, whether or not these behaviors have a label, such as ADHD, traumatic brain injury, emotional disturbance, or a specific learning disability. Like academics, student behaviors require differentiated approaches as students interact with the academics, themselves, and others.

In addition to differentiated approaches, Tom Hierck, Charlie Coleman, and Chris Weber (2011) advocate an approach that:

> Ensures that the dignity of the student is always paramount. Every student, regardless of background, ability, performance, or behavior, deserves to be treated with respect. How we treat our students—the language we use, the tone of voice we project, and the behavior we model—all have an impact on student behavior. (p. 56)

Both adults and students must exhibit appropriate behaviors to achieve a positive learning environment that promotes academic success.

PBIS focuses on improving the school and class climate and decreasing reactive classroom management (Sugai, 2016). Appropriate student behaviors maximize academic achievement. Like MTSS, PBIS screens all students and monitors progress. Screening involves structured observation and student-based data recording. For example, teachers note the number of times a student calls out or gets out of his or her seat, and then spins that to focus on the positive, such as when the student appropriately raises his or her hand, follows teacher directions, stays on task, and so on. These observations may involve tally marks, anecdotal notes, student logs, behavioral graphs, and home-school communications.

Appropriate student behaviors maximize academic achievement.

Observation helps teachers develop behavioral expertise. Just as oral fluency is required for successful reading strides or mathematics fluency is needed for improved calculation and problem solving, behavioral fluencies ensure increased efficacy and positive results for both students and teachers. Teachers should clearly communicate classroom rules and expectations, deliver effective instruction, respond to behavioral violations, and of course, reinforce appropriate student behavior (Reinke et al., 2013).

PBIS looks at the incidence and prevalence of inappropriate behaviors, their triggers, and ways to replace them with better choices and strategies. It moves from Tier 1 interventions for the whole class that offer expectations and procedures, to small-group secondary interventions at Tier 2 for at-risk students, and finally, to individualized tertiary interventions for higher risk students at Tier 3.

Figure 5.2 (page 102) offers examples of appropriate and inappropriate student behaviors.

Teachers must monitor students as they follow the rules for classroom discipline and exhibit appropriate social behavior during whole-class instruction, cooperative work, or peer interactions on the playground, in the hallway, or in the

Appropriate Behaviors	Inappropriate Behaviors
Raising hand in class	Calling out and being impulsive
Waiting his or her turn	Interrupting others
Following verbal and written directions for assignments	Ignoring classroom routines, structures, and rules
Focusing on task	Being inattentive and easily distractible
Staying in one's seat	Hopping around the classroom; fidgeting excessively
Complying with school rules and classroom structure	Defying authority and wanting his or her own way
Accepting and respecting differences	Displaying intolerance for any agenda or person other than own viewpoint and self
Offering a pleasant demeanor	Being irritable, unhappy, and moody
Being flexible and accepting environmental changes and other points of view	Being rigid or compulsive with an inability to do or see things through another perspective or lens
Seeking help from others	Ignoring peer and adult support
Taking the initiative with self-efficacy	Waiting to be told or corrected; little self-direction
Picking up on social cues to switch gears	Ignoring surroundings and the modeling of appropriate behavior of others
Providing positive responses to peer and adult interactions	Displaying challenging behavior; being out of sync with other classmates' and adults' needs

Figure 5.2: Examples of appropriate and inappropriate student behaviors.

lunchroom. Using PBIS, teachers first acknowledge behavioral issues, which then leads to identifying a baseline level of performance, with a plan to intervene and remediate. Monitoring progress, tweaking the interventions, and moving forward the plans for behavioral differences, like the academic interventions, must be specific to each student's learning needs.

Attention and Cooperation

When teachers give students a way to track their progress, this increases student attention in class. For example, they can monitor and guide students to correctly tally positive attending behaviors that are scribed in color-coded, dated charts to increase self-awareness and regulation. The reproducible "My Behavior Chart" (page 111) provides a chart where students can reflect on their behavior. The first box, *part of the time*, should be shaded red so

the student stops and thinks about how to improve his or her attention. While tally marks in the section *most of the time* are better, students still require improvement; it should be yellow. The last box should be green, *almost all the time*, signifying that a student is ready to move ahead as a focused learner.

At the end of each week, students count the tallies in each category and then share progress in weekly teacher-student conferencing. The goal is to increase student self-awareness and boost intrinsic motivation.

Teachers can also share candid photos they take in the classroom of students when they display attending behavior. Teachers can review a digital student-attending folder with students as a visual reminder of what positive behavior looks like to encourage appropriate, attending behavior. Positive reinforcement shapes and increases attending behavior.

Multiple Curriculum Entry Points

Teachers can minimize classroom disruptions when they honor and shape appropriate behaviors through various interventions and supports, including multiple curriculum entry points. This includes multisensory engagements, tiered instruction, and a collaborative problem-solving approach. These multiple curriculum entry points support academics and behavior with the appropriate instructional interventions.

The following sections offer strategies to ensure that inappropriate behavior is not the result of ineffective instruction.

Visual, Auditory, and Kinesthetic/Tactile Approaches

Behaviors such as impulsivity, inattention, and defiance can be linked to frustration caused by lessons that do not engage students in ways they learn best. VAKT approaches delivered during core instruction help students to better absorb literacy and mathematical skills and multidisciplinary concepts. Sometimes students struggle because teachers are almost exclusively instructing through verbal presentations or lectures. If verbal instruction is not a student's preferred mode of learning, then difficulties begin at a foundational level and spiral as the reading, mathematics, and other skills and concepts increase in complexity and become more abstract.

VAKT approaches can increase the skills of students with dyslexia (International Dyslexia Association, 2016; Jeyasekaran, 2015). Letter sounds come alive when students see, hear, trace, tap, and feel them. An Orton-Gillingham, structured, multisensory approach benefits the whole class as well as individual learners (Academy of Orton-Gillingham Practitioners and Educators, 2012).

If students don't reach fluency at Tier 1, teachers can instruct students within Tiers 2 and 3 to reinforce word decoding and reading comprehension with multisensory applications. VAKT includes literacy resources such as increased instructional videos, visual dictionaries, Wikki Stix, pipe cleaners, sandboxes, raised glue, digital games, and more. Mathematics manipulatives might include counting chips, Unifix cubes, foam dominoes, base-ten blocks, algebra tiles, geoboards, place-value disks, hundreds charts, decimal squares, and virtual tools.

Increasing VAKT strategies during instruction can help students across the curriculum. For example, students who are learning about the Louisiana Purchase might better understand the concept if the teacher displays a map showing how the United States doubled in size. Listening to text on digital platforms and conducting experiments solidify difficult scientific text. Proving Newton's second law with a hard-boiled egg and nylon pantyhose simulating a bungee cord's elasticity offers novelty that the brain seeks in order to concretize Newton's abstract concept into long-term memory. Students might be more engaged by watching one of Sal Khan's online instructional videos (www.khanacademy.org) explain how to solve a geometric theorem and periodically stopping the video to take notes.

Exploratory classrooms offer students ways to construct their learning and actively "play" with the concepts. Students can increase their focus and channel their impulsivity, rather than passively receive information while seated at their desks.

> *Exploratory classrooms offer students ways to construct their learning and actively "play" with the concepts.*

When students act out terms and concepts through gestures and movements, they can more easily remember and cement these concepts in their minds. VAKT strategies help increase memory and an understanding of abstract skills, concepts, and procedures. For example, if a student spins to demonstrate the earth's rotation around the sun or does a headstand to demonstrate an understanding of the meaning of *reciprocal* in mathematics when dividing fractions, then that student has literally done something to imprint that term or concept into long-term memory. The following MTSS lessons include VAKT strategies.

MTSS Lesson Connections

The following elementary, middle school, and high school lesson examples outline a multi-tiered system of supports that values differentiated instruction for academics and behavior. They infuse Pólya's four-step, problem-solving approach to (1) understand the scenario (identify student levels), (2) devise a plan (determine interventions), (3) carry out the plan (implement steps and monitor progress), and (4) reflect on performance (analyze students' responses to interventions) across the disciplines. RTI is a multifaceted process but never a problem if teachers collaborate with other school staff, students, and sometimes students' families to produce solutions.

Elementary Example

In this elementary lesson, students study cell structure and learn academic vocabulary associated with this science topic.

Understand the Scenario

This elementary class includes students with diverse literacy levels. In the lesson, students are learning about the parts of cells and their structures. When students receive a science assignment that requires reading or writing, several of them struggle to decode multisyllabic words and have difficulties with syntax. Students display varying levels of proficiency in class discussion and written expressions. This co-taught class has a general and a special education teacher. Weekly curriculum-based science assessments reveal that 80 percent of the class average proficient scores. The remaining students have varying prior science knowledge, interest, and motivation. Some students are distractible during whole-class instruction.

Devise a Plan

The general education science teacher consults with the school reading interventionist who observes the class and offers additional strategies that the special and general education teachers implement in small groups. These strategies include using graphic organizers to compartmentalize cell facts; implementing writing frames; directing explicit instruction on how to break up words into their affixes, root words, and syllables; and offering ways to improve syntax. The special and general education teachers decide to offer science instruction with the whole class, smaller skill-specific science groups, and individualized conferencing.

The teachers use ClassDojo (www.classdojo.com), an online behavior-management program, to increase positive classroom behaviors that, in turn, influence on-task science performance (for example, appropriate participation, attention, and persistence). ClassDojo allows students to receive increased behavioral feedback using avatars they create to represent themselves, which boosts interest and motivation. The teachers use these avatars to reward positive behavior such as active listening, class participation, helping others, and working hard. Overall, avatars are offered in virtual environments as a way to observe and imitate identities and situations that may differ from a real-life experience, but students can view, model, and replicate them (Yoon & Vargas, 2014). Some students may be quicker to respond to this type of virtual feedback than direct verbal praise or other forms of monitoring.

Carry Out the Plan

The teachers explain academic language and concepts in a step-by-step manner to make content comprehensible for all students. Supplemental instruction reviews the cell concepts, with students sorting ideas into similarities and differences using a Venn diagram. Science literacy goes beyond labeling cell parts with words, adding conceptual descriptions, such as anecdotal cell glossaries and visual representations, Cell Picture Show (www.cell.com/pictureshow), and hands-on investigations. Students then view and examine the online slides of cells that other students create or share on their own.

Teachers then offer the following instruction in Tiers 1, 2, and 3.

- ➤ **Tier 1:** Visuals—Teachers offer core instruction that includes multimedia presentations of cell parts, their functions, and the differences between plant and animal cells; PowerPoints; and curricular animations. Visuals depict how the cell vocabularies relate to each other, as shown in figure 5.3.

  These visuals generate discussion about the cell concepts, such as:

  - Cells are the basic units of life and work together to form tissues.

  - Tissues make up organs.

  - Organs work together to form systems.

- ➤ **Tier 2:** Multisensory activities—Teachers divide the class into smaller groups, and each group cooperatively creates 3-D cells with a choice of concrete objects to incorporate multisensory activities. For example, a plastic bag represents the cell membrane, gelatin represents the cytoplasm, a grape represents the nucleus, and candy sprinkles represent ribosomes.

- ➤ **Tier 3:** Decoding scaffolds—A small group of students listens to recordings of the science text. Following along in the text offers an auditory accompaniment to the visual representation to increase fluency, without allowing decoding difficulties to interfere with comprehension of science concepts. Other students have word boxes with the key vocabulary broken up into their syllables in a UDL approach (for example, *nu-cle-ous*, *mem-brane*).

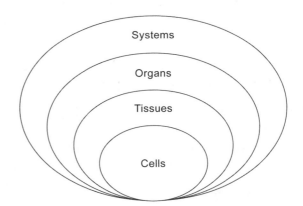

Figure 5.3: Cell vocabulary.

Reflect on Performance

Performance-based science assessments in this lesson include informal quizzes, interactive science journals, and responses to inquiry-based discussion. In addition, the teacher reviews cell projects and points earned on ClassDojo to offer academic and behavioral feedback with attention and social interactions during cooperative 3-D cell creations.

Middle School Example

Sometimes students display inappropriate behaviors in what they deem as less structured environments, such as art, music, or physical education classes. Sometimes a physical education class offers students a chance to show what they know without requiring written or reading requirements to interfere with performance. When educators ask students to share their favorite subject, many often select physical education as their first choice due to the active engagement. However, like other disciplines, physical education requires structured, four-step lessons that respond to learner levels.

Understand the Scenario

This middle school physical education class has twenty-six students. Seven have attention, memory, behavioral, emotional, and social issues, including distractibility, impulsivity, and difficulty interacting with peers. One student has a physical disability with limited mobility. According to the National Association for Sport and Physical Education (2000) guidelines, the teacher should provide ongoing formative and summative assessments to all students, including those with disabilities. This includes a baseline level describing how a player holds, shoots, passes, and dribbles the ball.

Devise a Plan

The physical education teacher speaks with the students' general education teachers to gather more background information on specific students' learning, physical, and emotional profiles. Together, the collaborative team shares prior student performances to formulate a plan

for moving forward to increase praise for positive behaviors and reinforce appropriate social interactions to establish consistent rules in all environments. The physical education teacher then designs instructional practices for skill development. Feedback is ongoing, specific, and timely (for example, step-by-step instructions with discrete task analysis of how to take a jump shot). The teacher offers the student with limited mobility verbal conferencing, peer mentors to navigate the court and perform the physical requirements, and physical opportunities to safely interact with peers on the team.

> *The collaborative team shares prior student performances to formulate a plan for moving forward.*

Carry Out the Plan

Teachers can use *Appropriate Instructional Practice Guidelines, K–12: A Side-by-Side Companion* (Society of Health and Physical Educators America [SHAPE America], 2009) in reference to learning environment, instructional strategies, curriculum, assessment, and professionalism as the core of the plan. This includes units of sufficient length and breadth that are appropriate for middle school–age students, along with small-sided games (one player versus one player, two players versus two players, and so on) and short activities that allow for ample opportunities to practice basketball skills.

Teachers then offer the following instruction in Tiers 1, 2, and 3.

> ➢ **Tier 1:** Instruction and modeling—The teacher offers instruction and modeling on the basketball rules, fouls, violations, and player positions. This includes foot

alignment, leg bending, hand positioning, arm angling, pivoting, and rebounding. Adapted physical education is student driven and more frequently monitored.

> **Tier 2:** Multitiered engagements—Students break into smaller groups and practice dribbling and passing. The teacher and instructional assistant circulate and monitor the smaller groups and video the students participating in basketball activities. (Teachers should always check and follow school policies on video procedures.)

> **Tier 3:** Personalized feedback—Students view themselves on video to rate their dribbling and passing, and notice foot alignment, leg bending, and more. The teacher intermittently stops the video for student critique; critique occurs in a classroom atmosphere that views constructive criticism as a growth opportunity. Meanwhile, some students work on rules and form, along with how to be a team player (for example, telling one student where to stand and how to assist). Students also view professional basketball videos as models. The teacher gives specific and individualized feedback (for example, stepping forward on the opposite foot when throwing the ball). Students with physical disabilities are not delegated to keep score but are taught how to be team players and safely share and apply the basketball knowledge.

Reflect on Performance

Data on student achievement serve two purposes for the teacher. They evaluate basketball for effective instruction and encourage students to compete against previous personal performance, rather than peers (for example, number of shots made and verbal and physical assists). Although this lesson does not focus on literacy and mathematics, it demonstrates the importance of related subjects in reference to the core. Physical education also provides a time to highlight interests and strengths and work with peers as a team, without literacy and mathematics struggles highlighted. This increases self-confidence among peers, who view each other as capable, which a hierarchy of reading and mathematics skills does not define.

High School Example

Geometry involves understanding concepts, such as symmetry, congruence, and similarity, and applying terms that include coordinates, transformation, and theorems. Some students who have less interest in mathematics, differing prior skills, and difficulties with visual perception cannot successfully apply the many geometric intricacies. That is when a collaborative, four-step, problem-solving approach can assist teachers in helping their mathematics students.

Understand the Scenario

In this high school class of twenty-five students, four struggle to apply geometric reasoning due to differing prior geometry experiences and fewer motivational and organizational skills. For example, they can identify the types of angles when they are isolated but have difficulty identifying, naming, and knowing angle properties and measurements when lines intersect in vertical, adjacent, and linearly paired angles outside of and within shapes. Several students also need support to apply the geometric principles in word problems. Finally, some students have varying mathematics interest and motivation in the subject, while others have difficulty managing their time and organizing their work.

Devise a Plan

The general and special education teachers and the mathematics interventionist gather as a collaborative team and select evidence-based instructional strategies that include direct instruction with teacher demonstration, guided practice, visual representations, verbal explanations, cognitive talk-alouds, ways to organize assignments, and methods for increasing study skills with self-management. The team also notes how it will intervene with mathematics strategies that address visual-spatial issues. Sometimes students identify difficulties to visually process information (Kelly, 2014). These learners may not be able to complete the geometric tasks since visualizing where objects are placed in a given space is challenging.

The team decides that more formal mathematics screening should occur three times during the year with an initial baseline level, mid-year review, and then a summative assessment. The team monitors students' mathematics progress for performance and skill gaps and perceptual concerns. Team members discuss the additional materials to proactively have available (for example, larger graph paper and compartmentalized mathematics frames). In addition, the team reviews six-week grade reports based on students' mathematics performances. Teachers provide and monitor time management and organizational supports each week with student–teacher conferencing and calendar and notebook checks.

Carry Out the Plan

Structure here is essential, as teachers share weekly objectives with students who are then privy to the master plan as active participants in their learning successes. This plan offers students step-by step mathematics goals, along with the appropriate behavior and organizational supports to help them achieve those goals.

Teachers then offer the following instruction in Tiers 1, 2, and 3.

➤ **Tier 1:** Structure, observation, and manipulatives—Explicit instruction includes sharing the schedule of mathematics goals with students at the beginning of each week.

- *Monday*—Types of angles (acute, right, obtuse)

- *Tuesday*—Measurement of angles with a protractor in polygons

- *Wednesday*—Vertical, adjacent, and linearly paired angles

- *Thursday*—Angle measurements within circle arcs

- *Friday*—Angle applications and celebrations (Celebrating mathematics successes with statements such as, "I now know how to . . . " This can be applied to other subjects as well to increase students' self-esteem and metacognition.)

Whole-class instruction includes ongoing observation and geometric tasks that offer concrete applications of the representational and abstract concepts (for example, creating acute, obtuse, and straight angles with chopsticks). The teacher gives students opportunities to manipulate geometric shapes in mathematics centers set up with activities using diverse materials (for example, tangrams, geoboards, chopsticks, tessellation art, and virtual manipulatives from Sketchometry [https://sketchometry.org/en/index.html]).

➤ **Tier 2:** Guided practice and peer modeling—The teacher, mathematics interventionist (as available), classmates, and online tutorials provide guided practice and modeling (for example, Khan Academy high school geometry [www.khanacademy.org/math/geometry] and Purplemath Quadrants and Angles [www.purplemath.com/modules /quadangs.htm]). Guided practice includes geometry lessons with academic strategies designed to increase motivation with closer proximity and repetition of concepts delivered in Tiers 2 and 3.

Peers, with teacher guidance, can act as tutors who offer practice in smaller groups. The teacher closely monitors the four students who are struggling to be certain they understand underlying concepts, such as identifying the vertex, naming an angle, applying the principles and facts for missing angle measurements of lines and within polygons, and understanding that vertical angles are opposite angles that intersecting lines form. The teacher also introduces, supports, monitors, and reinforces organizational skills.

➤ **Tier 3:** Manageable demands—The teacher arranges mini-conferences in which he or she gives students opportunities to review angle basics and can provide timely, corrective feedback, which guides performance and increases mathematics confidence and interest. The teacher chunks assignments into smaller parts with step-by-step discrete task analysis that ascertains prior student knowledge, such as knowing that the angles in a triangle measure 180 degrees.

The teacher divides weekly agendas into subskills for students as needed and provides smaller, manageable demands; regular observational and written checks; and more frequent feedback to be sure students are engaged in appropriate behaviors to achieve geometric tasks with mathematical fluency to apply angle properties.

Reflect on Performance

Teachers give both formative and summative assessments at regular intervals each week to ensure adequate progress and geometric fluency. The six-week check informs and drives instructional design for the following weeks. The mid-year assessment determines if additional remediation or enrichment is required.

The reproducible "Problem-Solving Approach: Turning Challenge Into Growth" (page 112) invites teachers to collaboratively devise a plan that responds to student performance levels. Teachers can use it to outline each of the four problem-solving steps to understand and respond to student challenges. Step one identifies a student's challenges—determining whether they are academic, behavioral, perceptual, and so on, and leads to the next step of devising a tiered plan for instruction. Step two compiles plans for the whole class, small groups, and individual students. Steps three and four invite teachers to respectively carry out the plan and then look back to collaboratively review the progress achieved to determine if the next steps involve enrichment or remediation.

Conclusion

Student behavior is connected to academics, and academics are connected to behavior. These elements do not exist in isolation, and one definitely influences the other. When implementing RTI, it's important that teachers do not leave behavior out of the equation, but instead, incorporate behavioral supports and interventions into the multitiered system of supports.

Quality core instruction at Tier 1 often prevents the need for more targeted and intensive instruction at Tiers 2 and 3. This chapter's lessons offered differentiated activities through quality instruction that transforms student challenges into solutions with step-by-step planning, appropriate pacing, and effective assessment.

> *Quality core instruction at Tier 1 often prevents the need for more targeted and intensive instruction at Tiers 2 and 3.*

As discussed, VAKT strategies concretize the abstract. For example, even though some science students have lower reading levels, the cell concepts in the elementary lesson remain accessible because the instruction includes increased visuals to strengthen decoding issues.

Listening alone is not enough for students to become adept at skills and concepts. Lecturing does not stimulate neurons; active learning experiences concretize concepts. People generally remember and learn by doing. The middle school physical education lesson is a good example of that, as students also pass, dribble, and shoot the ball.

In the high school geometry lesson, students learn through a step-by-step structure and increased collaboration; they share and own mathematics objectives. Ways to learn are not limited to the mathematics textbook or worksheets but occur within mathematics think groups, cognitive talk-alouds, face-to-face interactions, and digital tutorials.

To conclude, students have to be engaged in a myriad of ways, and teachers require time to plan quality instruction that includes opportunities to observe, record, plan, assess, and heighten student skills.

> *Students have to be engaged in a myriad of ways, and teachers require time to plan quality instruction.*

Chapter 6 continues the discussion on strategic engagements and outlines how to fine-tune and individualize instructional delivery to maximize student achievements.

My Behavior Chart

Name: _____

Directions: Complete this chart to describe your behavior this week.

Check the behaviors that apply.
- ☐ I had eye contact with the teacher or student who was speaking to me.
- ☐ I can repeat or paraphrase what I heard.
- ☐ I did not understand what to do next, so I asked for help.
- ☐ I achieved good results because I attended, listened, and responded.
- ☐ Other: _____

Part of the Time	Most of the Time	Almost All the Time

Days	My Reflections
Monday	
Tuesday	
Wednesday	
Thursday	
Friday	
Week Total	

I helped my peers today, when I _____
_____.

There was a disagreement, but then we _____
_____.

Together, our group _____
_____.

Problem-Solving Approach:
Turning Challenge Into Growth

Name: _____

Directions: Complete this chart to identify student challenges and opportunities for growth.

1. Identify the student's challenges. ☐ Academic ☐ Behavioral ☐ Communicative ☐ Perceptual ☐ Attention ☐ Organization ☐ Social ☐ Emotional ☐ Sensory ☐ Physical ☐ Other: _____	Comments:
2. Compile plans for the whole class, small groups, and individual students. ☐ Whole class ☐ Small groups ☐ Smaller groups and individual learners	Comments:
3. Carry out the plan.	Comments:
4. Collaboratively review progress and, if needed, plan enrichment and remediation.	Comments:

CHAPTER **6**

MINIMIZING AND MAXIMIZING STRATEGIC ENGAGEMENTS FOR RIGOROUS LEARNING

To get from one place to the next requires a strategic plan. In order for students to be successful, teachers must design this plan to achieve specific outcomes. Collecting data, determining levels, needs, and gaps; developing and implementing the plan; and then measuring performance are all parts of organizational change (Perron, Gomez, & Testa, 2016). RTI requires this same organization. Planning, intervention, and reflection are where instructional decisions respectively begin, arrive, and move forward.

This planning involves mapping out quarterly and monthly curriculum goals for sharing concepts and skills during the school year. As the year progresses, teachers can then refine this road map when reflecting on student progress, basing weekly and daily lessons on quarterly and monthly lessons, and then further breaking down those plans for each week and day.

Strategic engagements require active student involvement in the learning process. Passive learning does not create the sense of ownership that active engagement does. When students think about what they are doing, how they are doing it, and how to continually make improvements, then the strategies live within them, not their teachers. Strategic engagements yield internalization to value both the outcome and the ongoing process and strategies.

Minimizing student engagements does not mean the curriculum is diluted, just presented and approached differently. Maximizing student engagements does not mean students are frustrated, but it does mean that the learning objectives appropriately challenge them. Teachers must respond to diverse student needs to develop increased skills to rigorously and strategically engage with the concepts.

> *Minimizing student engagements does not mean the curriculum is diluted, just presented and approached differently.*

Rigorous learning in the classroom requires intentional effort and continual teacher reflection to create an engaging learning environment (Perron et al., 2016) that encourages students to organize, process, elaborate, and engage with the content with cognitively complex tasks (Marzano & Toth, 2014). Rigor is the underlying force that accompanies each teacher's journey to successfully navigate the core curriculum.

Figure 6.1 illustrates the structure of this chapter.

Challenge and Engage

Teachers should challenge and engage all students. Students need to be challenged but not frustrated. Both teachers and students reflectively gauge understanding through discussion and activities that invite critical thinking. Ultimately, engagement needs to meaningfully enrich all learners to explore what they now know and how they will continually grow and learn. Teachers can do this by minimizing and maximizing strategic engagements; pacing, repeating, and enriching instruction; and fine-tuning and individualizing instruction.

Minimize and Maximize

Core mastery requires student fluency with the academic content. Teachers can replace a skill-and-drill mentality with practices that challenge and engage students on their levels of learning to accomplish this (Marzano, 2007; Vander Ark & Schneider, 2014). Skill and drill usually means a teacher offers quick activities introducing a

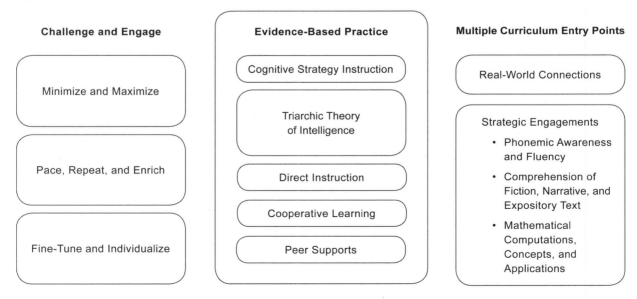

Figure 6.1: Plan for minimizing and maximizing strategic engagements for rigorous learning.

new skill and practices the skill until it becomes automatic. Responsive lesson pacing allows students the time to absorb concepts and practice procedural skills so they can own and apply the practices. At times, this means that the teacher must minimize the core to ensure students do not become frustrated. Or, the teacher can maximize the core to allow students to preview upcoming concepts, learning objectives, and ultimate outcomes. Some students require repetition, and some require enrichment.

> *Responsive lesson pacing allows students the time to absorb concepts and practice procedural skills so they can own and apply the practices.*

Teachers can minimize the core by presenting fewer concepts or requirements at one time, and he or she can maximize the core by increasing pacing and complexity. Strategic engagements must not overwhelm some students or disengage others.

For example, if students are writing a persuasive essay, the teacher might minimize by asking them to first write three solid paragraphs before writing the required eight. To maximize, the teacher might ask some students to write ten to twelve paragraphs. Students who work in an authentically open and supportive setting take more risks, face challenges head on, and cultivate genuine enthusiasm for learning (Perron et al., 2016).

The reproducible "KWL Chart" (page 131) provides a blank template that teachers can use to discover, monitor, and guide student knowledge. Figure 6.2 shows a completed example of this chart on the topic of endangered species. Students can complete this chart individually or in small groups. The chart promotes student empowerment and multiple representations, engagements, actions, and expressions, and requires both student and teacher signatures. Having co-teachers, interventionists, and assistants also sign sends a message to staff and students that everyone's voice is valued. KWL promotes accountability, invites strategic teacher-student partnerships, and guides next steps in the learning process.

Our KWL About Endangered Species		
Know	**Want to Learn**	**Learned**
What we know about endangered species:	What we want to know and will learn more about endangered species:	What we now know about endangered species: (Cite texts and online sources.)
Some animals are in trouble and may not live on the earth much longer.	How can we as humans help animals to survive?	We discovered that humans could make a difference for endangered species. For example, the bald eagle is no longer on the extinct animal list. We know that humans threatened the bald eagle's seashore habitat. If we cut down too many trees or overhunt, animals such as the bald eagle will face extinction. Source: Animal Fact Guide (n.d.)

Figure 6.2: Example of completed KWL chart.   continued →

To demonstrate our knowledge, we will:	Notes (help or resources that we need; staff assistance):
☑ Write a poem	Need extra time to read, an online spelling tool, and more breaks
☐ Draw a picture with a caption	Student signatures:
☐ Write bubble dialogue	*Ima Student*
☐ Create a digital product (for example, Quizlet, PowerPoint presentation, Kahoot! online book)	*Wanna Grow*
☐ Create a song or dance	Teacher and support staff signatures:
☐ Other	*Mr. Share Knowledge*
The bald eagle is a bird that can soar to heights	*Mrs. Letta Learn*
We humans cannot deny its rights	
Banning DDT helped their non-extinction fate	
Baby eaglets are in nests where they incubate	
So the mama and papa bald eagle say, "Please…"	
Don't cut down the trees!	

Pace, Repeat, and Enrich

Moving ahead means that instructional plans provide appropriate pacing, repetition, and enrichment. Students with diverse needs require engagement that instructs, yet challenges, with an allowance for adaptability and advancement. Pacing involves a Goldilocks approach (DeWitt, 2014), which applies the fairytale to appropriate instructional supports that are "just right" for students. This includes speed of delivery that holds student attention, yet aligns the content to students' levels. Since students are varied in their ways of thinking, teachers must account for these differences rather than denying or ignoring them (Gardner, 1995).

Each day, schools present varying challenges that involve other factors beyond student diversity. Interference with lesson-plan objectives can happen as a result of various reasons, ranging from an unscheduled evacuation drill to school assemblies to half days. Therefore, teachers must continually and flexibly implement pacing, repetition, and enrichment into lessons.

As an adjunct university professor, I supervise teacher candidates' fieldwork placements. Before they set foot in the classroom, the class must map out each quarter's concepts to provide appropriate pacing, repetition, and enrichment. When I introduced this task, many candidates were unhappy and felt overwhelmed. However, once they began mapping, they realized it was not so difficult, and it actually eased their planning for the entire year. When they entered the classroom, delivering the core was not as challenging, since they referred back to the quarterly and monthly planners. Mapping out lesson ideas each month and each quarter offers a look at the big picture and allows teachers to add more repetition or enrichment based on student data. This big picture then assists with weekly and daily lesson planning.

Many school districts have curriculum pacing guides and lessons that plan out the entire year and each month at a glance. As an educator and an inclusion coach, I design and share mapping plans. Figure 6.3 and figure 6.4 (page 119) are examples of quarterly and long-range monthly lesson plans I designed with the preservice teachers I supervised. I adopted these examples from models in *Inclusion Lesson Plan Book for the 21st Century* (Karten, 2012), classroom visits, and student communications. These student-tested lesson plans offer opportunities for both repetition and enrichment and can be applied across disciplines and subjects.

Figure 6.5 (page 119) shows an example of grade 9 monthly lesson plans for English.

Teachers can use the reproducibles "Quarterly Lesson Planner" (page 132) and "Long-Range Monthly Planner" (page 133) to map out their curriculum for the year, noting the content in each quarter and month. They should think about the curriculum but also include emotional, social, behavioral, communicative, and study skills.

Teachers can review student responses to mapped-out goals to provide enrichment and

First-Quarter Goals and Objectives	**Mathematics:** Increase basic mathematics facts for whole numbers with addition, subtraction, multiplication, and division facts and place value to the billions place.
	Language arts: Express written thoughts in a coherent paragraph for intended audience in a personal narrative and friendly letters.
	Reading: Identify story elements—characters, setting, plot, climax, and resolution.
	Science: Learn about the food chain with producers, consumers, and decomposers.
	Social studies: Create a time line of U.S. history events on explorers.
	Perceptual: Attend to teachers and peers, filtering out distracting stimuli.
	Social and behavior: Follow all classroom and school rules with academics and behavior (for example, homework, attention, time on task).
	Study skills: Organize work in assignment pads and calendars for short-range and long-term assignments.
Second-Quarter Goals and Objectives	**Mathematics:** Apply computational skills to solve one- and two-step word problems with whole numbers using all operations.
	Language arts: Improve writing with descriptive vocabulary, transitional words, and *wh-* expanders in three-paragraph reports and essays. (Instruct on ways that the *who, what, where, when,* and *why* questions expand written expressions.)
	Technology: Explore keyboard skills with word documents, implementing language and spelling tools.
	Reading: Work cooperatively in literature circles as artists, passage pickers, word wizards, and connectors across selected fiction and nonfiction texts.
	Science: Identify plants' and animals' needs and explore vertebrate and invertebrate classification.
	Social studies: Introduce current events by reviewing articles in TIME for Kids; explore life in early New England and the Middle and Southern colonies.
	Social and behavior: Assist peers with assigned cooperative roles in stations and centers; follow all established rules.
	Study skills: Learn how to outline information from science and social studies texts using headings as guides.
Third-Quarter Goals and Objectives	**Mathematics:** Solve computations and word problems with decimals, fractions, and whole numbers.
	Language arts: Proofread writings in descriptive essays, using rubrics, samples, and input from peer and teacher conferences.
	Reading: Understand the characters' motives and the event sequencing.

Figure 6.3: Grade 5 quarterly lesson plans.

continued →

	Science: Observe daily weather and investigate the water cycle, erosion, and weathering.
	Social studies: Outline events leading to the American Revolution.
	Communication and world languages: Write to pen pals overseas.
	Social and behavior: Increase self-awareness through tallying on-task behavior.
	Study skills: Create mnemonics and acrostic sentences for concepts in English, social studies, mathematics, and science.
Fourth-Quarter Goals and Objectives	**Mathematics:** Apply geometric principles and solve ratio, proportion, and probability problems.
	Language arts: Apply figurative language in writings and to publish selected works from writing journals.
	Reading: Accurately answer oral and written inferential questions in fiction and nonfiction genres.
	Science: Explore plate tectonics with convergent, divergent, and transform fault boundaries.
	Social studies: Explore the U.S. government, westward expansion, and immigration in the nineteenth through early twentieth centuries.
	Technology: Create PowerPoint presentations on science and social studies units.
	Social and behavior: Exhibit social reciprocity in all classroom activities and school interactions with peers and adults.
	Study skills: Monitor progress in all content areas through reviewing graphed grades in portfolios.

Source: Adapted from Karten, 2012.

Month	Action
August	Review IEP and 504 plans with teams and share accommodations with all staff. (Children are eligible for accommodations under a 504 plan if they have a physical or mental health disability that limits one or more major life functions.)
	Offer a class survey on multiple intelligences, like the Scholastic (Connell, n.d.) "Multiple Intelligence Questionnaire" (http://bit.ly/2I0TCvA), to gain more information about students' likes and interests. Share school rules and daily schedules.
September	Review map skills to identify locations of continents and oceans. Introduce the scientific process, literature circles with short stories, study skills, following directions, and mathematics skills with whole numbers.
October	Write planners and expanders, review outlines, establish reading logs, practice keyboarding, begin taxonomy project, create monster reports, and model mathematics problem solving.
November	Review cultural awareness, introduce logic boxes, meet students for progress conferences, organize food collections, begin unit on persuasive essays, and introduce two-digit multiplication.
December	Study poetry unit, read the novel *The Phantom Tollbooth* by Norton Juster, work in cooperative catalog mathematics shopping groups, organize community projects, and reinforce creating mnemonics.
January	Review class graphs of favorites (books, movies, sports, foods), create science vocabulary picture books, form social studies centers on graphic regions, read *Old Yeller* by Fred Gipson in literature groups, and write essays and poems.
February	Create heart bulletin board, study figurative language, review idioms, complete analogies, begin fraction unit, work in technology centers, begin colonial projects, and connect fractions to decimals.
March	Study tessellations, review probability, create and interpret graphs, design individual/cooperative inventions, begin unit on women in history, read Dr. Seuss books, perform American Revolution play, and review mathematics problem-solving strategies.

April	Study architecture unit, introduce lights and shadows, begin geometry unit, and review all computation skills, branches of government, ratio, and proportions.
May	Complete hands-on algebraic equations, create a classroom newspaper, and do the Holocaust unit. Read *Terrible Things: An Allegory of the Holocaust* by Eve Bunting and *The Upstairs Room* by Johanna Reiss for the Holocaust unit.
June	Read James Lincoln Collier and Christopher Collier's *My Brother Sam Is Dead*; conduct research for biography reports; have students keep exercise logs; reinforce reading, mathematics, and cooperative social/emotional skills in sports and mathematics centers; introduce area and perimeter; and review compare and contrast skills students learned from September to now.
July	Study home and environment units: beaches, rainforests, coral reefs, forests, mountains, grasslands, deserts, and freshwater; self-assess portfolios to review work samples, quizzes, and mathematics, science, reading, and social studies performance tests.

Source: Adapted from Karten, 2012.

Figure 6.4: Grade 5 long-range monthly lesson plans.

Months	Action
September–November	Introduce and explore persuasive writing. Teach students about brainstorming to come up with a successful argument and write a persuasive essay with an introduction, thesis statement, at least three supportive paragraphs with evidence, and a conclusion.
	Teach students what makes a short story a specific genre. Explore setting, point of view, audience, characters, and themes. Students read and examine short stories over the next three months.
December–February	Students start a journal by writing impressions of the novels they are reading with teacher input on grammar and style. Students discuss and explore a novel's major elements. Explore setting, point of view, character development, and themes. Students read *Frankenstein* by Mary Shelley and then *To Kill a Mockingbird* by Harper Lee.
March–April	Students differentiate among and identify the following types of poetry: sonnet, blank verse, nursery rhymes, haiku, pastoral, and imagery. They write five poems over a two-month period. Explore the works of T. S. Eliot, Emily Dickinson, Ezra Pound, Robert Frost, Sylvia Plath, Christina Rossetti, Maya Angelou, Walt Whitman, Langston Hughes, and Edgar Allan Poe. Review Poetry 180 (www.loc.gov/poetry/180) for a list of poets and selections.
May–June	Students read and contrast short passages of Shakespearean plays, writing how the comedies and tragedies relate to modern-day life. Students work in groups to read the play *Julius Caesar* and use persuasive skills to write an argument about the events to present to the class. Afterward, students participate in a mock trial of Julius Caesar. Students read *A Midsummer Night's Dream*.

Figure 6.5: Grade 9 English monthly lesson plans.

repetition. For example, teachers should continually apply and reinforce study skills taught in the first week of school. For example, students will not hone any learned mathematics skills if they never apply these skills during the school year. Hence, teachers should look ahead and look back as they pace lessons and consider how to repeat the learning for those students who need reinforcement or enrichment. As educators, we also know that a rigorous learning journey includes the necessary supports and interventions that help but do not enable students nor create learned helplessness.

Fine-Tune and Individualize

When someone plans a trip, there are many decisions to make at the onset, during the journey, and when the journey is over. Skilled navigators and seasoned travelers plan, reflect, and fine-tune the itinerary. Likewise, students of all ability levels require fine-tuning that values the core's integrity, student levels, and skilled instructors. Rigor is the navigating force that propels effective and finely tuned instruction.

> *Students of all ability levels require fine-tuning that values the core's integrity, student levels, and skilled instructors.*

In education, the zone of proximal development helps students learn to complete tasks that are slightly more difficult than ones they cannot complete independently (New World Encyclopedia, 2013; Wass & Golding, 2014). Teachers should offer some more difficult concepts at a higher ability level to provide novelty, rigor, relevance, and retention.

Similarly, Csikszentmihalyi's positive flow view of psychology and how students achieve goals emphasizes the importance of deep concentration and challenge (Beard, 2015). This differs from a teaching approach that spoon-feeds students with a skill-and-drill mentality. Fine-tuning the core instruction means providing enriching lessons that go beyond reciting basic concepts verbatim.

Students need to extend learning to meaningful applications. For example, if a student fails to demonstrate mastery of reading comprehension during whole-class instruction, then the teacher can fine-tune these skills in a small, guided reading group, as the rest of the class completes more demanding reading and language tasks. A student who cannot demonstrate proficiency in multiplying whole numbers by fractions may require more fine-tuning on the properties of fractions before more complex steps frustrate him or her as procedural requirements increase. Ultimately, assistance should lead to independence with increased confidence, based on prior instruction and experiences.

Evidence-Based Practice

This section presents research on how students learn to learn. Rigor begins in the early grades and is not exclusive to one group of students. Beginning in kindergarten, if teachers fail to bring their students to core proficiency levels, then teachers in the next grades are even more challenged to get their students to achieve the required grade-level benchmarks (Bowden, 2015).

Deeper learning occurs when students know how to self-regulate achievements and behavior (Ning, 2016). It is crucial to offer students immediate, realistic feedback on their performances to provide them opportunities to develop more awareness or metacognition of the rigorous requirements. For example, in the primary grades, students can improve mathematics skills through problem solving, listening, and word-association activities that include a focus on metacognition and working memory (Cornoldi, Carretti, Drusi, & Tencati, 2015). During secondary grades, metacognitive instruction can lead to better self-regulated learning outcomes (Zepeda, Richey, Ronevich, & Nokes-Malach, 2015). Therefore, teachers can maximize rigor with increased learner metacognition.

Twenty-first century students require instruction that recognizes but does not penalize students who may not immediately learn concepts with automaticity or behave perfectly under teacher direction the first time. Evidence-based practices acknowledge different types of learners and theories on how students acquire intelligence, whether they are applying practical, analytic, or creative skills (Sternberg, 2014). Practices such as cognitive strategy instruction, triarchic theory, direct instruction, cooperative learning, and peer supports assist students with diverse learning needs. These practices are the rigorous driving forces that acknowledge differences but provide the vehicles for learning.

Cognitive Strategy Instruction

Alfred W. Tatum (2011), dean of the College of Education and director of the University of Illinois at Chicago Reading Clinic, advocates that a truly differentiated classroom honors learner diversity; students are constantly growing and changing as they participate in learning activities. He recommends practices such as:

> ➤ Making connections between instruction and students' experiences

> ➤ Fostering student autonomy

> ➤ Providing strategic grouping

> ➤ Implementing research-based cognitive strategy instruction (CSI)

CSI includes a self-regulated strategy development model that facilitates improved performances of struggling students (University of Nebraska-Lincoln, College of Education and Human Sciences, 2016). Rigor cannot exist in a vacuum without student ownership and self-awareness of responsibilities. Simply put, teachers are facilitators of the navigation, not the drivers. Students who are aware of the steps and processes formulate strategies and goals that lead to academic and behavioral gains. Teachers can use KWL charts,

student conferencing, observational data, increased verbal instruction, modeling, and guided practice to facilitate this performance. CSI ultimately empowers and qualifies students to recognize how they own and shape their learning.

As Sternberg's (2000) triarchic theory of intelligence demonstrates, analytic, synthetic, and practical factors are an essential part of the rigorous cognitive conversation.

Triarchic Theory of Intelligence

Sternberg, a cognitive psychologist and psychometrician, outlines three levels of intelligence. *Analytic intelligence* means that students understand the components of a problem. *Synthetic intelligence* refers to insight, creativity, intuition, and how one handles novel situations. *Practical intelligence* applies both the analytic and synthetic skills to solve everyday problems.

Sternberg's (2000) theory gives intelligence a broad definition and relates to how students with and without exceptionalities learn. It is important to note that the terms *disability* and *exceptionality* comprise a diverse spectrum that includes students who possess these intelligences. A label of *disability* can never overshadow this fact.

The acronymic sentence in figure 6.6 (page 122) outlines the thirteen disability classifications under the Individuals With Disabilities Education Act (IDEA) legislation, which ensures that students with disabilities receive a free and appropriate education (Karten, 2014): **A**ll **v**ery **d**etermined **s**tudents **d**eserve **i**nfinitely **m**ore **o**pportunities **t**han **s**chools **h**ave **e**ver **o**ffered.

*All **very** **determined** students **deserve** **infinitely** **more** **opportunities** than schools **have** ever **offered.***

Each student with an IEP receives services under IDEA. This thirteen-word acronymic sentence outlines the thirteen IDEA classifications:

All **v**ery **d**etermined **s**tudents **d**eserve **i**nfinitely **m**ore **o**pportunities **t**han **s**chools **h**ave **e**ver **o**ffered.

Autism	Deafness-blindness	Traumatic brain injury
Visual impairment (including blindness)	Intellectual disability	Speech and language impairment
Deafness	Multiple disabilities	Hearing impairment
Specific learning disability	Other health impairment	Emotional disturbance
		Orthopedic impairment

Source: Karten, 2014.

Figure 6.6: Thirteen IDEA classifications.

Within each disability classification, students have strengths and gifted areas. Gifted students do not have a monopoly on critical-thinking skills, nor should a disability prevent a student from exploring his or her gifts. Background knowledge differs, but students with and without IEPs can obtain academic fluency through core instruction. Rigor is an essential ingredient that helps construct knowledge for students of all ability levels.

Direct Instruction

Teachers can achieve rigor through a variety of instructional models, including direct skill instruction. Direct instruction introduces, repeats, and enriches the core curriculum. Teachers can use direct instruction to teach concepts such as learning sight words, including more descriptions in writings, improving reading comprehension, and understanding algebra. Direct instruction says, "Here are the facts and the steps you need to follow. Now follow them." Ongoing practice, modeling, and feedback are important elements to combine with direct instruction (Botts, Losardo, Tillery, & Werts, 2014; Kanfush, 2014).

When teachers provide direct instruction, differentiation is key. Direct instruction offers concepts and skills to students, but it needs to honor each student's skill level (National Institute for Direct Instruction, n.d.). Direct instruction also offers guidance, modeling, practice, and application. Teachers introduce concepts and then allow students the time to complete planned activities to internalize the learning.

Direct instruction says, "Here are the facts and the steps you need to follow. Now follow them."

However, when a student creates a skit or song on a novel or science concept, writes his or her own three-paragraph essay, or solves a multistep word problem with discussion, then he or she is applying instruction to produce tangible products that serve as evidence of learning. A combination of instructional choices does not dilute direct instruction but enhances it with multiple and responsive learner engagements. Rigor, therefore, is not defined by one type of engagement but must be differentiated and responsive to each student's skill sets.

Cooperative Learning

Cooperative learning offers students opportunities to improve both social and academic skills and the supportive classroom mentalities that replace competition. When students learn cooperatively, they work together as a team toward a common goal. Students usually enjoy teamwork. Cooperative learning is not a separate entity; teachers should combine cooperative learning with other small-group and whole-class instruction.

For example, some students might work in a small group with guided instruction from an interventionist to practice and apply multiplication knowledge, while other students work on the same or different assignments individually or cooperatively. For example, they might quiz each other on mathematics facts or apply multiplication principles to challenging word problems. How teachers structure student-to-student interaction has a lot to say about how well students learn, how they feel about school and their teachers, how they feel about each other, and how much self-esteem they have (Johnson & Johnson, n.d.). Cooperative learning adds a level of rigor as students learn to interact with one another to problem solve, increase responsibility for learning, work constructively, and manage tasks (Gilles, 2016).

Robert E. Slavin (2014) writes that cooperative learning is not party time for students but requires structure. Interdependence with positive interactions and individual accountability are essential. Often the structure includes assigning student roles. For example, teachers can assign numbers to students in each group and then randomly call one number. The selected student must respond to a question to demonstrate individual and group progress (Slavin, 2014). This structure prevents just one student being the one who owns the learning. Cooperative learning is about sharing and gaining knowledge, not monopolizing learning.

If a student needs help to cooperatively and rigorously complete assignments with peers, teachers can try the following.

➢ Divide the rules into discrete steps. Instead of saying, "Work together as a team," outline specific behavioral expectations with student examples and nonexamples of how to effectively listen to peer voices.

➢ Ask the student to rephrase his or her responsibilities as an individual within the group and then as a cohesive member. For example, the materials person in a cooperative mathematics group gathers the manipulatives, distributes them to each person in his or her group, and then collects and returns the materials to a designated location.

➢ Distribute a rubric for cooperative work expectations that has a rating scale. For example, include time on task, followed directions, shared insights, valued input of others, and completed academic requirements. Communicate that the work is cooperative, but the grading is individualized.

How teachers structure student-to-student interaction has a lot to say about how well students learn.

➢ Begin the cooperative group session with a short lesson for the whole class on student voices (for example, how to be a peer who agrees that it is okay to respectfully disagree). Float to cooperative groups to offer more proximity and verbal praise for appropriate cooperative roles, and infuse gentle reminders as needed.

➤ Ask students to complete brief reflective exit cards on individual and group contributions and happenings after each class, ensuring increased metacognition of cooperative work practices. For example, I helped my peers today, when I _____. There was a disagreement, but then we _____. Together, our group _____.

Peer Supports

Minimizing and maximizing strategic engagements for rigorous learning mean thinking about how students learn with each other and from each other, and how they help one another navigate tasks and accept and apply help from peers. Peer supports include collaborative learning, cross-age peer support, and peer modeling (Riester-Wood, 2015). Collaborative learning asks students to practice and review concepts together. Cross-age peer support generally involves older students helping younger ones, such as middle school students assisting elementary students with reading and writing, or high school students tutoring and assisting younger grade levels. Peer modeling helps students with academics and presents positive role models for school and classroom routines and expectations.

Students with and without disabilities gain many skills such as advancements with academics, friendships, and character development. Students gain skills, whether they are giving or receiving help, as they learn to view diversity through a positive lens and increase their learning. Students can transfer and apply these interactions to life outside the classroom since peer modeling is a tool that shows evidence of proactively preventing behavioral problems (Richards, Heathfield, & Jenson, 2010). As students mature, these experiences shape a foundation that yields positive attitudes toward diversity, increased self-esteem, and higher acceptance of future coworkers.

Multiple Curriculum Entry Points

If learning is not connected to real life outside the classroom, students might forget isolated facts a moment or two after handing in an assessment. They might rigorously study for a test but internalize and absorb very little unless assignments and assessments are connected to relatable, real-world concepts. The strategic engagements in this section are pragmatic and strategic to connect the school day with students' lives both inside and outside the classroom. Navigating the core requires that rigor is not limited to textbooks, but connected to multiple engagements, individualization, and student interests.

> *If learning is not connected to real life outside the classroom, students might forget isolated facts a moment or two after handing in an assessment.*

Real-World Connections

Once students have foundational knowledge of a topic, they need to apply it to real-world situations, such as reading and following directions, comparing and contrasting opinions, and calculating tips or discounts. RTI advocates ongoing plans to improve literacy and mathematics skills, which are accomplished through multiple entry points. Models and functional connections that go beyond the written words on a worksheet and the traditional classroom lecture style are what students remember. Students respond to structure, but the core needs to be delivered with novelty and cognitive ownership to ensure retention and real-world connections. Branching out beyond the classroom develops higher-level thinking skills, but this also includes rigorous, strategic instructional interventions.

Students who are lifelong learners deepen their knowledge to transfer the learning to real-world situations. This transference includes exploring unfamiliar ideas and developing the intellectual habits that make the skills and concepts meaningful (Fisher & Frey, 2016). Carol Ann Tomlinson (2016) writes that the mileposts of a meaningful life include producing quality work, creating one's own happiness, taking time to know oneself, being kind, demonstrating responsibility, teaming with other people, learning to challenge oneself to think deeply, and playing with the learning.

Students must continually pursue knowledge as they navigate life's many roads. Ultimately, learners' metacognition of where they are now, where they want to go, and how they will get there requires deeper reflection. Teachers and families scaffold, guide, compact, and reinforce learners when they provide them with the appropriate learning experiences and resources.

Rigorous instructional interventions value and connect to real-world applications. In mathematics, teachers might relate decimals to money or baseball batting averages to establish real-world connections. Teachers might investigate climate changes with environmental weather connections for students who can read fiction books such as *Cloudy With a Chance of Meatballs*; *The Lion, the Witch and the Wardrobe*; or *The Call of the Wild*. Learning relates to real-world explorations that expand words from the page to the environment in which students live.

Strategic Engagements

The following strategic engagements offer ways for students to understand literacy and mathematics, own their learning, and hone skills in three ways: (1) phonemic awareness and fluency; (2) comprehension of fiction, narrative, and expository text; and (3) mathematical computations, concepts, and applications. These lessons also offer important opportunities for repetition, enrichment, and rigor.

Phonemic Awareness and Fluency

Teachers begin with whole-class instruction in Tier 1 and then offer additional levels of instruction in Tiers 2 and 3. Note that multisensory instruction and progress monitoring occur in all three tiers.

Students in all tiers collect words they learn on monthly vocabulary lists and move from group to group sharing with peers as they cooperatively create celebratory paragraphs with the new vocabulary. Teachers can offer word exploration contests; ask students to be vocabulary sleuths to record and share specific types of words (for example, *v-e words* or words with three syllables); and post class A–Z word charts, where students can write a word learned beside its corresponding first letter.

Students who demonstrate proficiency engage in phonemic activities that advance their levels. Teachers should challenge students to go beyond identifying rhyming words to add rigor as they produce rhymes in short verse and poems.

Additional practice to decode multisyllabic words across the disciplines includes more challenging prefixes and affixes, such as comparing *circle* to *circular*, *circumference*, and *circuitous*; *skeleton* to *endoskeleton* and *exoskeleton*; and *comprehend* to *comprehension* and *incomprehensible*. Students also identify and examine words in classroom and school signs.

Tier 1

Teachers screen students to determine which *phonemes* (smallest sound unit in spoken words) they hear, identify, and manipulate. They can achieve this with informal reading inventories that assess student knowledge of short and long vowel sounds, consonant sounds, digraphs, diphthongs, *r*-controlled vowels, and additional special sounds (for example, /zh/ in *vision*). Teachers provide direct instruction with scaffolding and appropriate pacing with oral and written instruction and systematic practice using:

> ➢ Rhyming words
> ➢ Syllable segmentation
> ➢ Sound substitution
> ➢ Sound isolation
> ➢ Phonemic segmentation

Younger students in grades 1–4 can record progress with color-coded bar graphs to visually see their advancements on specific subskills. Older students in grades 5 and beyond can plot x and y coordinates and calculate their weekly mean successes to record their progress.

Tier 2

Smaller groups of students, scoring less than 80 percent mastery, receive multisensory instruction three times each week for sixty-minute sessions to increase awareness of phonemic progress with letter sounds in syllables and words. Generally, Tier 1 offers strong evidence-based classroom instructional practices that allow 80–90 percent of students to achieve success, without further intervention required. Tier 2 offers strategies to approximately 5 to 10 percent of the student population who require this additional assistance (Searle, 2010).

Guided direct practice to fluently read sentences develops more automaticity. Explicit and systematic instruction should include how to decode and encode real and pseudo words and syllables. Students graph progress with specific phonemes and word fluency achieved on color-coded bar graphs, recording words read correctly per minute with a variety of genres that include both fiction and nonfiction text.

Tier 3

School reading specialists and speech-language pathologists provide students who require more assessment, review, and additional phonemic strategies with daily consultation and intervention.

Comprehension of Fiction, Narrative, and Expository Text

Teachers provide multitiered engagements with comprehension skills for whole-class, small-group, and one-to-one instruction to teach and guide, yet promote independence and application across genres.

Teachers offer opportunities to vary reading purposes with independent and cooperative assignments at Tiers 1, 2, and 3. They provide opportunities for rigorous text application, transfer, and generalization within ongoing classroom centers and libraries, such as poetry corners. Teachers can use curriculum-related articles, magazines, newspapers, cookbooks, how-to-manuals, high-interest reading series, and online articles.

They then invite students to record understandings, reactions, and personal thoughts about text read in interactive notebooks and reading journals.

For enrichment, teachers challenge students to read and paraphrase both fiction and nonfiction text with increased annotations and note-taking tools and skills. They have students read and compare different selections on the same topics and settings with similar formats in both fiction and nonfiction texts to ascertain characters' and authors' points of view. They then ask students to create their own comprehension questions featuring cause and effect, sequencing, prediction, inference, and so on.

Tier 1

Teachers offer direct-skill, whole-class instruction using the features, similarities, and differences of fiction and nonfiction high-quality text. For fiction, teachers ask students to sequence, retell, predict, make inferences, draw conclusions, and summarize fiction text. Fiction texts include realistic, historical, science, myth, fantasy, graphic novels, novellas, and first-person to third-person narrative. They provide instruction that covers characters, setting, plot development, resolution, and summarizing.

For nonfiction, teachers model skills across the genres to inform, explain, and entertain. Examples include studying memoirs versus current events or science articles; increasing prior knowledge; and identifying title, headings, table of contents, preface, index, illustrations, captions, charts, maps, glossary, and more. Tier 1 includes providing graphic organizers, digital recordings, speech to text, and how to cite text-based evidence.

Tier 2

Teachers provide direct instruction with vocabulary, plot, and text organization (for example, signal and transitional words, chronology, plot development, character actions and consequences, word choice, and sensory elements that describe people, events, and settings). They instruct small groups four times each week for thirty- to forty-minute periods to explore inclusions and omissions of facts and events authors share, with direct and implied thoughts communicated and inferred. Scaffolding includes the same comprehension skills with text on differing reading levels (for example, Dolch readers, *Newsela*, *TweenTribune*).

Tier 3

Teachers offer daily cloze reading instruction that discusses and synthesizes shorter and longer text excerpts. They retell the main ideas in fiction and expository texts, and work with Reading A–Z (www.readinga-z.com) resources—downloadable, projectable teacher materials for reading instruction. (Visit **go.SolutionTree.com/RTI** to access live links to the websites mentioned in this book.) Teachers provide students with comprehension passages that include examples and nonexamples of on-target responses. They discuss strategies on how to find, support, and cite responses with text-based evidence and how details shape information, themes, and plots with students. This tier should also include ongoing collaboration with reading specialists and instructional support teams for which additional resources to use and ways to help students to own the skills.

Mathematical Computations, Concepts, and Applications

Mathematics lessons teach calculation, estimation, mental computation, number sense, whole numbers, operations, money, time, measurement, geometry, probability, statistics, fractions, decimals, percentages, ratios, proportions, algebra, patterns and relationships, and real-world applications.

Reviewing prior mathematics concepts with students promotes automaticity. Research indicates that students with lower mathematics skills require more repetitions than more skilled students (Burns, Ysseldyke, Nelson, & Kanive, 2015). Tiered instructional practice offers review time to strengthen prior concepts. Reinforcing what students know means that specific feedback with examples and nonexamples accompanies informal and formal mathematics checks. Response repetition produces higher acquisition of mathematics facts and correct computation for students with intellectual disabilities (Rapp et al., 2012).

> *Reinforcing what students know means that specific feedback with examples and nonexamples accompanies informal and formal mathematics checks.*

Benson's (2012) mantra from the special education world, "Again, and again, and again and again," emphasizes useful repetitions. Some students are challenged by the rigorous academic concepts and life's circumstances; they need the responsive repetition that offers specific and guiding feedback. Repetition does not mean that the same mathematics texts and worksheets are used over and over again. Teachers need to implement responsive interventions that utilize a variety of resources.

RTI tiers are the framework for multiple response repetition. This repetition does not negate the rigor desired; it just helps navigate the journey. For example, Tier 2 might review and practice

concepts offered in core instruction, while Tier 3 might offer additional and more targeted remediation and additional time to achieve mastery. The idea is that teachers can support core instruction with increased exposure to reinforce learning for students with weaker skills.

Teachers must also challenge students with effective questioning that deepens thinking skills. High expectations with engaging mathematics centers offer ways to live-dream mathematics. Students have opportunities to solve with mathematics reasoning, such as following a recipe, planning and application. Examples include these:

> ➤ Determining a fair way to share of pretzels with five friends
>
> ➤ Figuring out a grade on a test if students know the number of questions answered correctly
>
> ➤ Planning a playground within a given space
>
> ➤ Doubling and halving recipes

When teaching mathematical computations, concepts, and applications, teachers should do the following at each tier.

Tier 1

Combine what learners know with ongoing computational drills and celebrations of students' learning milestones, transforming *I never liked mathematics* mentalities to *I can* statements. Mathematics representations for all tiers include those that are numerical, graphical, symbolic, verbal, and pictorial. Teachers provide the whole class with multisensory, step-by-step explanations and concrete and visual representations. Figure 6.7 illustrates that two addends equal a sum.

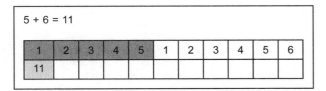

Figure 6.7: Addition visual.

Figure 6.8 provides a grid students can use to increase their multiplication skills by shading in the grid to equal the product.

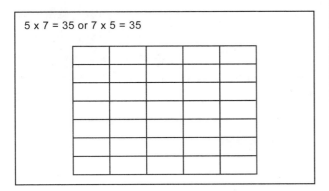

Figure 6.8: Mathematics grid.

Figure 6.9 shows an activity in which students use jelly beans to understand how to solve an algebraic equation. Students place two jelly beans on each plate to show x in the equation $4x = 8$, solving for x as 2. The jelly-bean approach may present a more palatable way for students to view algebra since something fun (jelly beans) now represents the numbers on the page. Students can act out similar jelly-bean problems in small groups.

If learners do not achieve the algebraic understanding within Tier 1, teachers should provide additional support in Tiers 2 and 3.

Tier 2

Teachers can provide a small group of students with discrete task analysis that includes formal and informal mathematics probes occurring three times each week to determine the exact part of a calculation or problem that each student does not understand (for example, adding the whole number to the numerator when converting mixed numerals to improper fractions). They can guide and monitor students during independent and small-group practice to ensure that errors are not repeated in calculations and word problems. Teachers talk through their thought process and provide guided practice and specific feedback. They also offer ongoing, real-life applications that allow students to recognize, value, and apply their mathematics achievements, and give frequent cumulative reviews.

Tier 3

Teachers can provide mathematics instruction that reinforces, models, and acts out word problems with skits, tutorials, and daily fluency drills to achieve automaticity of basic facts, calculations, and concepts. Instruction stresses patterns and generalizations that connect word problems to scenarios on student interest levels (for example, music, animals, and sports). Students solve multiple problems using the same strategy. Mathematics and special education teachers then offer interventions and consultations.

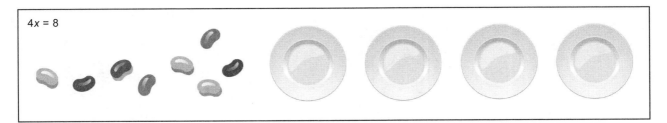

Figure 6.9: Jelly-bean algebra.

Conclusion

In conclusion, this chapter demonstrates that scaffolding, guiding, compacting, and reinforcing the core requires a Goldilocks or "just right" approach that minimizes and maximizes the curriculum to connect to individual student skill sets, without losing the rigor. Teachers maximize instruction when they prepare and encourage students to own the strategies through challenge, engagement, fine-tuning, and real-world connections. When teachers introduce the core with strategic engagements and the appropriate pacing, students can apply, stretch, and translate the concepts to achieve inside and outside the classroom.

> *Teachers can provide mathematics instruction that reinforces, models, and acts out word problems with skits, tutorials, and daily fluency drills to achieve automaticity of basic facts, calculations, and concepts.*

The final chapter explores how we can ensure professional fidelity and integrity within the learning environment. Teachers must not only adequately understand and prepare for RTI, but administrators must provide supp... development and ... practices and stud...

KWL Chart

Our KWL about _____.

Know	Want to Learn	Learned
What we know about	What we want to know and will learn more about	What we now know about (Cite texts and online sources.)

To demonstrate our knowledge, we will:

☐ Draw a picture with a caption

☐ Write a poem

☐ Offer bubble dialogue

☐ Create a digital product (for example, Quizlet, PowerPoint presentation, or Kahoot! online book)

☐ Create a song or dance

☐ Other

Notes (help or resources that we need; staff assistance):

Student signatures:

_____

_____

_____

_____

Teacher and support staff signatures:

_____

_____

_____

Quarterly Lesson Planner

First-Quarter Goals and Objectives	
Second-Quarter Goals and Objectives	
Third-Quarter Goals and Objectives	
Fourth-Quarter Goals and Objectives	

Long-Range Monthly Planner

Month	Action

CHAPTER 7

ENSURING PROFESSIONAL FIDELITY

Professional fidelity means answering questions such as researchers Michele Meyer and Linda Behar-Horenstein (2015) propose: (1) How does RTI affect teacher learning? (2) What new practices are required of teachers during RTI implementation? and (3) How can school and district leaders best support teacher problem solving under an RTI model? A professional and responsive RTI toolbox provides teachers with access to the hands-on resources to address these questions and provide the interventions needed to ensure student learning at all levels.

Resources such as flowcharts, graded word lists, and appropriately leveled texts, and supports such as determining which research-based practice is appropriate for individual learners, are essential parts of the RTI journey. Time, collaborative efforts, and fidelity to professional practices strengthen multitiered academic and behavioral interventions. Teacher fidelity to RTI allows the

responsive learning experiences to occur at each tier, over time, and across disciplines.

Navigation requires mapping out a course of action. Administrators, teachers, families, and students are collaborative partners. The foundation of implementing RTI successfully requires administration to guide and support teachers to work together as a team by observing each other, offering feedback, questioning, supporting, and valuing how to navigate various interventions in their classrooms. Overall, RTI provides prevention and early intervention, but this cannot occur without professional fidelity and collaborative supports.

Teachers can strengthen their instruction when they are armed with effective strategies and resources, which include meaningful professional development. Teachers are professionals who want their students to succeed, but they require the administrative support of school and district leaders, tools, time, and supports to plan, intervene, collaborate, and reflect on how to make this happen. Figure 7.1 illustrates the structure of this chapter.

Professional Development

Effective professional development is at the core of RTI. Professional development is similar to RTI, because professional development is also multitiered, with whole-group, small-group, and individual opportunities for teachers to learn. This includes support for planning time, discussions, research, and student reviews at large faculty meetings and trainings, within small groups, and with individual staff and additional collaborative stakeholders. Meaningful communications, engagements, and reflections help all staff and students to learn and grow together, individually and collectively. Teachers can then apply this new knowledge to whole-class core instruction and multitiered practices.

An effective RTI program requires effective leadership as the integral voice that communicates, collaborates, facilitates, creates, and reinforces expectations and best practices. School leaders must provide teachers with adequate professional development and training and time to review the data, analyze student progress, tweak plans, and collaboratively move forward with academic and behavioral objectives (Buffum et al., 2009).

In the past, both special and general educators were used to doing their own thing when planning instruction and assessment. However, best practices in RTI require collaboration to collect and review data, deliver appropriate multitiered interventions, and implement teaming strategies for effective decision making (Burns et al., 2013).

Buffum et al. (2009) share that "RTI can help harness, systematically and coherently, the resources and expertise of specialists in general education, Title I education, English-language learner education, and special education" (p. 23). However, this cannot occur without ongoing and grounded professional development.

Effective leadership is key, as school leaders must support and provide the resources and professional development teachers need to implement RTI with fidelity. Figure 7.2 and figure 7.3 (page 138) illustrate how leadership is not delivered top-down but collaboratively, with the students always at the instructional core. Leaders are part of the collaborative team and should provide teachers with the appropriate tools and training to successfully embrace RTI strategies in their classrooms.

Teachers who provide the universal, secondary, and tertiary interventions require knowledge, preparation, and training on how to deliver the interventions with fidelity to RTI. Teachers struggle with the RTI implementation when they are uncertain of their job roles, how to manage interventions, and how to effectively utilize the data to make instructional decisions (Meyer

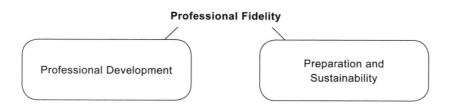

Figure 7.1: Plan for ensuring professional fidelity.

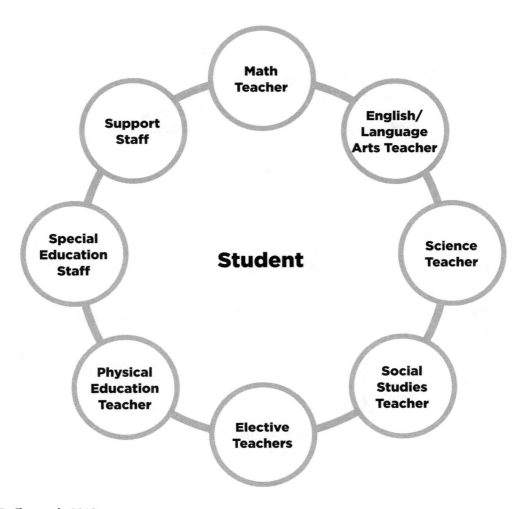

Source: Buffum et al., 2012.

Figure 7.2: 360-degree view of student learning at Tier 2.

& Behar-Horenstein, 2015). The RTI Action Network offers fidelity checklists (Kovaleski, n.d.; http://bit.ly/2kn4u5c), which provide engagement and observation tools for teachers to use for documenting the RTI steps required in areas such as vocabulary, comprehension, phonics, and other domains.

> *Professional development for RTI includes valuing teachers as individuals who have their own interests and teaching styles.*

Professional development for RTI includes valuing teachers as individuals who have their own interests and teaching styles. However, collaboration plays a major role, which means forming teams to gather information, select interventions, and determine which interventions are the most effective. Informed decisions are based on the data. Together, general and special education and instructional support staff review and select ways to plan, monitor, and share student progress. In order for RTI to be effectively delivered, administrative supports must promote professional development to ease, not burden, teachers so they can instruct diverse student populations.

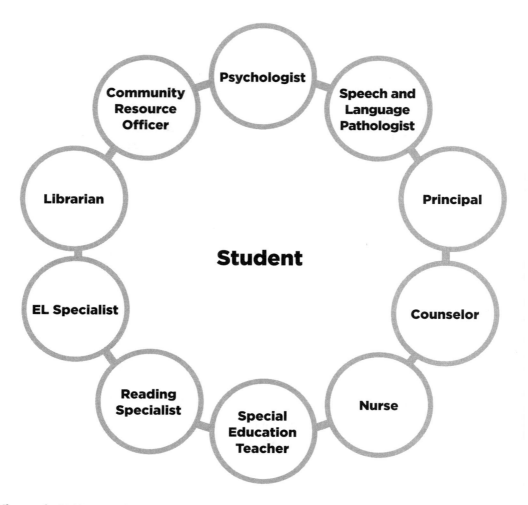

Source: Buffum et al., 2012.

Figure 7.3: 360-degree view of student learning at Tier 3.

Another form of support for teachers is coaching, which focuses on collaborative instructional decisions regarding who is on the journey, where you will go, and just how you will get there. Two types of coaching methods include supervisory and side by side (Kretlow & Bartholomew, 2010; Schnorr, 2013).

In supervisory coaching, the coach observes the teacher implementing a new strategy, records data on implementation of desired behaviors, and provides targeted feedback on strengths and opportunities for improvement following the lesson. Supervisory coaching is proven effective for improving academic instruction (Fisher, Frey, &

Lapp, 2011; Menzies, Mahdavi, & Lewis, 2008; Morgan, Menlove, Salzberg, & Hudson, 1994; Rudd, Lambert, Satterwhite, & Smith, 2009). In side-by-side coaching, the coach provides feedback to teachers during a lesson and may offer immediate comments on teacher behaviors observed and intervene or model an instructional practice during a lesson.

Administration must explore multitiered ways to help teachers become lifelong collaborative learners, problem solvers, and decision makers, regardless of teachers' experience, age, and general or special education university preparation. They should monitor teachers as they progress, with ongoing conversations and active coaching. Just as students are diverse, so are teachers. Teacher fidelity to responsive learning experiences ensures that RTI is *effective at each tier.*

Preparation and Sustainability

Teachers must receive the physical and emotional supports and tools they need to teach students at all levels. In addition, teachers must continually reflect on how to deliver the curriculum, offering fidelity to students and evidenced-based practices. RTI sustainability and generalization are imperative (Burns et al., 2013). This means that RTI monitoring is only valid if it is accurately communicated, ongoing, and effectively applied.

Sustainability at the school level involves pragmatic applications that support teacher preparation with buy-in, supports, collaborative practices, and fidelity to the process over time and across disciplines. For example, if teachers only try a strategy for one week, that is not proof that the strategy is either effective or ineffective. Learning is evolutionary. If a student is not succeeding with a given strategy, it's imperative to determine whether the teacher is applying the intervention accurately or if the student is just not responding well before abandoning the intervention.

Teachers must also be sure to create alignment between the tiers and an assessment of the effectiveness at each tier. At times, school personnel more consistently assess fidelity of implementation for Tier 2 interventions, but do not assess the fidelity at Tier 1 (Burns et al., 2013; Hill, King, Lemons, & Partanen, 2012).

Learning is evolutionary.

Professionalism requires behavioral changes for both teachers and administrators (Sarason, 1996). A survey of special education directors found that the most common supports for RTI implementation provided by state departments of education were short-term trainings and professional development (Werts, Lambert, & Carpenter, 2009). RTI is not an add-on, quick fix, or new sports model to try out but an essential element within the context of the school and for individual classrooms, students, and teachers.

How teachers and support staff implement the multiple tiers, what they look like, and the professional development needed to get there are all crucial elements. RTI routes are therefore planned and traveled with caution, scrutiny, and optimism. The RTI components are all important ones, but changes should be made in increments rather than all at once (Grimes, Kurns, & Tilly, 2006).

RTI routes are therefore planned and traveled with caution, scrutiny, and optimism.

Staff should work together to answer proactive questions such as which tools to use, how often to use them, and who will monitor progress (Wood, Goodnight, Bethune, Preston, & Cleaver, 2016). For example, teachers, reading interventionists, and literacy coaches might work together to decide if reading or mathematics progress is monitored once or twice a week or bimonthly. Realistic decisions require realistic planning. In addition, no teacher needs or wants to be overwhelmed by decisions that they have not been involved in from the onset.

The following are the core professional development parameters to help teachers and interventionists organize and reflect on their roles, screening process, and strategies for each tier of instruction in RTI.

Professional development should support teachers in gaining knowledge about:

- ➤ Student level of performance
- ➤ Screening required
- ➤ How to monitor progress
- ➤ Evidence-based instructional practices
- ➤ Evidence-based assessment practices
- ➤ Differentiated instructional approaches
- ➤ Student–teacher interactions
- ➤ Whole-class interventions
- ➤ Small-group interventions
- ➤ Individual interventions
- ➤ Team supports

Teachers and other staff can use the reproducible "Parameters for Professional Development" to help them reflect on the parameters they establish in their school.

Conclusion

The main goal of RTI is for each and every student to learn, no matter what his or her skill level or challenges. This starts with the school staff. Effective and ongoing professional development is key to helping teachers understand how to work together to implement a multitiered system of supports with fidelity. This also requires administration to support school staff by providing the needed training to deliver RTI with the greatest success. A driver, ship captain, and pilot all require training to navigate the roads, waters, and skies. Teachers require the same training and preparation to help their diverse learners navigate the core curriculum.

Parameters for Professional Development

Increase knowledge of:	Individual reflections:
☐ Student level of performance	
☐ Screening required	
☐ How to monitor progress	
☐ Evidence-based instructional practices	
☐ Evidence-based assessment practices	
☐ Differentiated instructional approaches	
☐ Student–teacher interactions	
☐ Whole-class interventions	
☐ Small-group interventions	
☐ Individual interventions	
☐ Team supports	
☐ Other: _____	

Collaborative reflections or comments:

EMBRACING RTI

Diversity enriches the world. Some students' contributions are not attainable, unless those students are allowed the opportunity to learn in a way that values who they are and who they can be. Not everybody learns the same way, but given the opportunity to shine, differences do not need to translate into deficits. If we embrace RTI with multiple entry points for core instruction, then students will be more responsive in school settings and beyond.

> *Not everybody learns the same way, but given the opportunity to shine, differences do not need to translate into deficits.*

Successful people are not always high achieving in school settings. For example, many people with dyslexia or reading challenges figured out ways to read because they received interventions offering these learning opportunities. So, it is evident that given these opportunities, students can become more confident and competent both inside and outside the classroom. When they become aware of how they learn best, students can translate that knowledge into future success.

Kevin O'Leary's verbal and critical-thinking skills are admirable; he did not permit his reading challenges to circumvent his achievements. Instead, he learned to discover his strengths (DyslexiaHelp, n.d.). Carol Greider, an American molecular biologist and Nobel Prize winner for discovering the enzyme *telomerase*, was in remedial classes due to her dyslexia. She thought she couldn't learn as well as others. However, she also kept thinking of ways to succeed, regardless of her reading difficulties. Some learners, like Greider, are good memorizers; but they may be poor spellers. Thomas Edison, Harvey Cushing, Danny Glover, Michael Phelps, Charles Schwab, Whoopi Goldberg, and Henry Winkler are just a few people who had difficulties in school but learned to gain knowledge in ways that allowed academics to be a part of the core ingredient to achieve ongoing successes (Yale Center for Dyslexia and Creativity, n.d.).

Successful outcomes have multiple entry points delivered within an RTI framework. Lessons throughout this book offered multiple entry points to gain core skills, including varied pacing, materials, and engagements that respond to student diversity. Teachers must present the curriculum in ways that honor diverse student levels and skill sets with high expectations for all. They should set up time in the lessons for review with on-level and challenging assignments to prevent inappropriately leveled work from leading to frustration, large academic gaps, and inappropriate student behaviors.

Success involves more than academics; it is a result of quality instruction, positive behaviors, problem-solving approaches, and collaboration. Any given classroom could include students with IEPs, students who are gifted, students who are considered average, students who speak English with more or less proficiency, students who are twice exceptional, students living in poverty, and students who have many degrees of physical, emotional, and financial supports.

Navigating the core curriculum with success requires planning, individualization, fine-tuning, collaboration, and rigor to reach all these students. It also requires a collaborative belief and effort that

each and every student, no matter what his or her challenges, can and will achieve when teachers provide appropriate interventions with fidelity. Collaboration must involve all staff, administrators, families, and most important, students.

Success involves more than academics; it is a result of quality instruction, positive behaviors, problem-solving approaches, and collaboration.

RTI offers the prevention and interventions that embrace how to teach students with a structured responsive plan. It is a viable and rigorous vehicle that traverses the multileveled core terrain. Safe travels as you successfully use RTI as your vehicle to navigate the core curriculum to support your students on the road to success.

REFERENCES AND RESOURCES

Academy of Orton-Gillingham Practitioners and Educators. (2012). *The Orton-Gillingham Approach*. Accessed at www.ortonacademy.org/approach.php on October 17, 2016.

Accessible. (2016). In *Dictionary.com*. Accessed at www.dictionary.com/browse/accessibility?s=t on October 12, 2016.

Achieve. (2015). *Closing the expectations gap: 2014 annual report on the alignment of state K–12 policies and practice with the demands of college and careers*. Washington, DC: Author.

Achievement. (2016). In *Dictionary.com*. Accessed at www.dictionary.com/browse/achievement?s=t on October 12, 2016.

Airth, M. (n.d.). *Pólya's four-step problem-solving process*. Accessed at http://study.com/academy/lesson /Pólyas-four-step-problem-solving-process.html on January 31, 2017.

American Federation of State, County and Municipal Employees. (n.d.). *Immigrants and immigration: Answering the tough questions*. Accessed at www.afscme.org/issues/immigration/resources/document /ToughQuestionsonImmigration-OneAmerica.pdf on July 11, 2016.

American Folklore. (2014). *Mexican folklore: Mexican fairytales*. Accessed at http://americanfolklore.net /folklore/2010/07/mexican_fairytales.html on July 11, 2016.

American Folklore. (2016). *Tall tales*. Accessed at http://americanfolklore.net/folklore/tall-tales on July 12, 2016.

American Masters. (2006). *Edgar Allan Poe: Terror of the soul—About Edgar Allan Poe*. Accessed at www.pbs.org/wnet/americanmasters/edgar-allan-poe-about-edgar-allan-poe/681 on July 12, 2016.

American Society for Horticultural Science. (2011, April 4). Student confidence correlated with academic performance, horticultural science class study finds. *ScienceDaily*. Accessed at www .sciencedaily.com/releases/2011/04/110404105901.htm on July 8, 2016.

American Speech-Language-Hearing Association. (2016). *Typical speech and language development.* Accessed at www.asha.org/public/speech/development on October 12, 2016.

Anderson-Lopez, K., & Lopez, R. (2013). Let it go. [Recorded by I. Menzel]. On *Frozen: Original motion picture soundtrack* [CD]. Burbank, CA: Disney.

Andrelchik, H. (2015). Reconsidering literacy in the art classroom. *Art Education, 68*(1), 6–11.

Animal Fact Guide. (n.d.). *Animal facts.* Accessed at www.animalfactguide.com/animal-facts on February 3, 2017.

Ask Smithsonian. (2016, February 26). Why do flamingos stand on one leg? *Smithsonian TweenTribune.* Accessed at www.tweentribune.com/article/tween56/why-do-flamingos-stand-one-leg on July 11, 2016.

Averill, O. H., & Rinaldi, C. (2011). Multi-tier system of supports. *District Administration, 48*(8), 91–94.

Bandura, A. (1994). Self-efficacy. In V. S. Ramachandran (Ed.), *Encyclopedia of human behavior* (Vol. 4, pp. 71–81). New York: Academic Press.

Barrett, P., Zhang, Y., Moffat, J., & Kobbacy, K. (2013). A holistic, multi-level analysis identifying the impact of classroom design on pupils' learning. *Building and Environment, 59,* 678–689.

Bas, G. (2016). The effect of multiple intelligences theory-based education on academic achievement: A meta-analytic review. *Educational Sciences, 16*(6), 1833–1864.

Basham, J., Israel, M., Graden, J., Poth, R., & Winston, M. (2010). A comprehensive approach to RTI: Embedding universal design for learning and technology. *Learning Disability Quarterly, 33*(4), 243–255.

Bauer, B. J. (2013). *Improving multiplication fact recall; interventions that lead to proficiency with mathematical facts* (Graduate research paper 11). Accessed at http://scholarworks.uni.edu/cgi/viewcontent.cgi?article=1011&context=grp on February 5, 2016.

Baumann, J. F., & Graves, M. F. (2010). What is academic vocabulary? *Journal of Adolescent and Adult Literacy, 54*(1), 4–12.

Beard, K. S. (2015). Theoretically speaking: An interview with Mihaly Csikszentmihalyi on flow theory development and its usefulness in addressing contemporary challenges in education. *Educational Psychology Review, 27*(2), 353–364.

Beck, I. L., McKeown, M. G., & Kucan, L. (2002). *Bringing words to life: Robust vocabulary instruction.* New York: Guilford Press.

Begeny, J. C., Laugle, K. M., Krouse, H. E., Lynn, A. E., Tayrose, M. P., & Stage, S. A. (2010). A control-group comparison of two reading fluency programs: The Helping Early Literacy with Practice Strategies (HELPS) program and the Great Leaps K–2 reading program. *School Psychology Review, 39*(1), 137–155.

Bender, W. N. (2012). *Differentiating instruction for students with learning disabilities: New best practices for general and special educators* (3rd ed.). Thousand Oaks, CA: Corwin Press.

Benedict, A. E., Park, Y., Brownell, M. T., Lauterbach, A. A., & Kiely, M. T. (2013). Using lesson study to align elementary literacy instruction within the RTI framework. *TEACHING Exceptional Children, 45*(5), 22–30.

Benner, G. J., Kutash, K., Nelson, J. R., & Fisher, M. B. (2013). Closing the achievement gap of youth with emotional and behavior disorders through multi-tiered systems of support. *Education and Treatment of Children, 36*(3), 15–29.

Benson, J. (2012). 100 repetitions. *Educational Leadership, 70*(2), 76–78.

Beyond the Darkness Publications. (2010, August 18). *Edgar Allan Poe—The raven—Read by James Earl Jones* [Video file]. Accessed at www.youtube.com/watch?v=WcqPQXqQXzI on July 12, 2016.

Bill and Melinda Gates Foundation. (2015). *Teachers know best: Making data work for teachers and students.* Seattle, WA: Authors.

Blachowicz, C. L. Z., & Fisher, P. (2000). Vocabulary instruction. In M. L. Kamil, P. B. Mosenthal, P. D. Pearson, & R. Barr (Eds.), *Handbook of reading research* (Vol. 3, pp. 503–523). Mahwah, NJ: Erlbaum.

BlackPast.org. (2015). *African American history: Primary documents.* Accessed at www.blackpast.org /african-american-history-primary-documents on October 12, 2016.

Blackwell, L. S., Trzesniewski, K. H., & Dweck, C. S. (2007). Implicit theories of intelligence predict achievement across an adolescent transition: A longitudinal study and an intervention. *Child Development, 78*(1), 246–263.

Blanton, L. P., Pugach, M. C., & Boveda, M. (2014). *Teacher education reform initiatives and special education: Convergence, divergence, and missed opportunities* (Document No. LS-3). Gainesville: University of Florida, Collaboration for Effective Educator, Development, Accountability, and Reform Center. Accessed at www.smcoe.org/assets/files/about-smcoe/superintendents-office /statewide-special-education-task-force/Teacher-Education-Reform-Initiatives-and-Special -Education-Convergence-Divergence-and-Missed-Opportunities.pdf on February 7, 2017.

Botts, D. C., Losardo, A. S., Tillery, C. Y., & Werts, M. G. (2014). A comparison of activity-based intervention and embedded direct instruction when teaching emergent literacy skills. *Journal of Special Education, 48*(2), 120–134.

Bowden, J. (2015). The Common Core's first casualty: Playful learning. *Phi Delta Kappan, 96*(8), 33–37.

Boyles, N. (2012). Closing in on close reading. *Educational Leadership, 70*(4), 36–41.

BrainPOP Educators. (n.d.). *Lesson ideas: Vikings.* Accessed at https://educators.brainpop.com/bp -topic/vikings on July 12, 2016.

BrainPOP Jr. (n.d.). *Social studies: Biographies—Johnny Appleseed*. Accessed at http://jr.brainpop.com /socialstudies/biographies/johnnyappleseed/preview.weml on July 12, 2016.

BrainyQuote. (n.d.). *Herbert Spencer quotes*. Accessed at www.brainyquote.com/quotes/quotes/h /herbertspe109568.html on February 2, 2017.

Brame, C. (2013). *Thinking about metacognition*. Nashville, TN: Vanderbilt University, Center for Teaching. Accessed at https://cft.vanderbilt.edu/2013/01/thinking-about-metacognition on October 12, 2016.

Bridges-Rhoads, S., & Van Cleave, J. (2016). #theStandards: Knowledge, freedom and the Common Core. *Language Arts, 93*(4), 260–272.

Brittain, B. (1983). *The wish giver: Three tales of coven tree*. Cambridge, MA: Harper & Row.

Buffum, A., Mattos, M., & Weber, C. (2009). *Pyramid response to intervention: RTI, professional learning communities, and how to respond when kids don't learn*. Bloomington, IN: Solution Tree Press.

Buffum, A., Mattos, M., & Weber, C. (2010). The why behind RTI. *Educational Leadership, 68*(2), 10–16.

Buffum, A., Mattos, M., & Weber, C. (2012). *Simplifying response to intervention: Four essential guiding principles*. Bloomington, IN: Solution Tree Press.

Burns, M. K., Egan, A. M., Kunkel, A. K., McComas, J., Peterson, M. M., Rahn, N. L., et al. (2013). Training for generalization and maintenance in RtI implementation: Front-loading for sustainability. *Learning Disabilities Research and Practice, 28*(2), 81–88.

Burns, M. K., Riley-Tillman, T. C., & VanDerHeyden, A. M. (2012). *RTI applications: Academic and behavioral interventions* (Vol. 1). New York: Guilford Press.

Burns, M. K., Ysseldyke, J., Nelson, P., & Kanive, R. (2015). Number of repetitions required to retain single-digit multiplication facts for elementary students. *School Psychology Quarterly, 30*(3), 398–405.

Butler, S., Urrutia, K., Buenger, A., Gonzalez, N., Hunt, M., & Eisenhart, C. (2010). *A research synthesis: A review of the current research on vocabulary instruction*. Washington, DC: National Reading Technical Assistance Center. Accessed at www2.ed.gov/programs/readingfirst/support /rmcfinal1.pdf on October 12, 2016.

Carnegie Mellon University. (n.d.). *Whys and hows of assessment: Formative vs summative assessment*. Accessed at www.cmu.edu/teaching/assessment/howto/basics/formative-summative.html on October 12, 2016.

Castek, J., & Beach, R. (2013). Using apps to support disciplinary literacy and science learning. *Journal of Adolescent and Adult Literacy, 56*(7), 554–564.

Castillo, J. M., March, A. L., Tan, S. Y., Stockslager, K. M., Brundage, A., McCullough, M., et al. (2016). Relationships between ongoing professional development and educators' perceived skills relative to RtI. *Psychology in the Schools, 53*(9), 893–910.

Center for Applied and Special Technology. (2011). *Universal design for learning guidelines version 2.0.* Wakefield, MA: Author. Accessed at www.udlcenter.org/sites/udlcenter.org/files/updateguidelines2_0 .pdf on October 21, 2016.

Center on Response to Intervention at American Institutes for Research. (n.d.a). *Essential components of RTI.* Washington, DC: Author. Accessed at www.rti4success.org/essential-components-rti on November 1, 2016.

Center on Response to Intervention at American Institutes for Research. (n.d.b). *Screening tool chart.* Accessed at www.rti4success.org/resources/tools-charts/screening-tools-chart on January 2, 2016.

Chace, W. M. (2015). What I have taught—and learned. *The American Scholar, 84*(10), 38–47. Accessed at https://theamericanscholar.org/what-i-have-taught-and-learned/#.V4OjcdIrJph on July 11, 2016.

Chandler, K., Fortune, N., Lovett, J. N., & Scherrer, J. (2016). What should Common Core assessments measure? *Phi Delta Kappan, 97*(5), 60–63.

Charles, R. I. (2005). Big ideas and understandings as the foundation for elementary and middle school mathematics. *Journal of Mathematics Education Leadership, 7*(3), 9–21.

ChildFun. (2016). *Mexico themed activities for kids.* Accessed at www.childfun.com/themes/world/mexico on October 12, 2016.

Cisneros, S. (n.d.). *Eleven.* Accessed at http://my.ccsd.net/userdocs/documents/qP2lEuWcYaAQAtMW .pdf on March 1, 2016.

Classroom Clipart. (n.d.). *Vikings clipart and graphics.* Accessed at http://classroomclipart.com/clipart /Clipart/Vikings.htm on February 3, 2017.

Coleman, D., & Pimentel, S. (2012). *Revised publishers' criteria for the Common Core State Standards in English language arts and literacy, grades 3–12.* Accessed at www.corestandards.org/assets /Publishers_Criteria_for_3-12.pdf on July 11, 2016.

Colorado Department of Education. (2008). *Literacy framework: Purposeful, direct, explicit, and systematic instruction.* Denver, CO: Author.

Colorín Colorado. (2015). *Selecting vocabulary words to teach English language learners.* Accessed at www.colorincolorado.org/article/selecting-vocabulary-words-teach-english-language-learners on October 12, 2016.

Common Sense Media. (n.d.). *All teen and kid member reviews for* Frozen. Accessed at www .commonsensemedia.org/movie-reviews/frozen-0/user-reviews/child on February 3, 2017.

Compton-Lilly, C. (2011). By the book and behind-the-glass: Teacher self-regulation in one reading intervention. *Language Arts, 88*(6), 429–438.

Connell, J. D. (n.d.). *Multiple intelligence questionnaire.* Accessed at https://printables.scholastic.com /shop/prcontent/Multiple-Intellgence-Questionnaire/9780439590204-001 on February 3, 2017.

Cornell University Library. (2016). *Evaluating web pages: Questions to consider—Categories.* Accessed at http://guides.library.cornell.edu/evaluating_Web_pages on October 12, 2016.

Cornoldi, C., Carretti, C., Drusi, B., & Tencati, C. (2015). Improving problem solving in primary school students: The effect of a training programme focusing on metacognition and working memory. *British Journal of Educational Psychology, 85*(3), 424–439.

Coulter, G., & Lambert, M. C. (2015). Strategic keyword instruction: Increasing fluency in connected expository text. *Reading Improvement, 52*(4), 133–141.

Council for Exceptional Children. (2014). *Council for Exceptional Children standards for evidence-based practices in special education.* Arlington, VA: Author.

Cunningham, B. (n.d.). *What's the difference between RTI and MTSS?* Accessed at www.understood.org /en/school-learning/special-services/rti/whats-the-difference-between-rti-and-mtss on May 28, 2016.

Curriculumbits.com. (2007). *Virtual dice.* Accessed at www.curriculumbits.com/prodimages/details /maths/mat0005.html on February 3, 2017.

Curwood, J. S., & Cowell, L. L. H. (2011). iPoetry: Creating space for new literacies in the English curriculum. *Journal of Adolescent and Adult Literacy, 55*(2), 110–120.

Darrow, A.-A. (2015). Differentiated instruction for students with disabilities: Using DI in the music classroom. *General Music Today, 28*(2), 29–32.

de Jager, B., Reezigt, G. J., & Creemers, B. P. (2002). The effects of teacher training on new instructional behavior in reading comprehension. *Teaching and Teacher Education, 18*(7), 831–842.

de Saint-Exupéry, A. (1943). *The little prince.* New York: Harcourt, Brace & World. Accessed at www .angelfire.com/hi/littleprince/framechapter21.html on January 30, 2017.

DeWitt, P. (2014). *The Goldilocks' principle: Meeting the needs of special education students* [Blog post]. Accessed at http://blogs.edweek.org/edweek/finding_common_ground/2014/09/the_goldilocks _principle_meeting_the_needs_of_special_education_students.html on November 8, 2016.

DyslexiaHelp. (n.d.). *Success story: Kevin O'Leary.* Accessed at http://dyslexiahelp.umich.edu/success -stories/kevin-oleary on March 15, 2017.

Education World. (n.d.). *Once upon a time: Lessons for teaching about fables, fairytales, folktales, legends, myths, tall tales.* Accessed at www.educationworld.com/a_lesson/lesson/lesson279.shtml on October 12, 2016.

Ehren, B. J. (2013). Expanding pockets of excellence in RTI. *The Reading Teacher, 66*(6), 449–453.

Every Student Succeeds Act, 20 U.S.C. § 6301 *et seq.* (2015).

Faggella-Luby, M., & Wardwell, M. (2011). RTI in a middle school: Findings and practical implications of a Tier 2 reading comprehension study. *Learning Disability Quarterly, 34*(1), 35–49.

Fanning, E. (2016). *Examination of the impact of students' skill levels on the effectiveness of evidence-based interventions for improving mathematics fluency.* Doctoral dissertation, City University of New York. Accessed at http://academicworks.cuny.edu/gc_etds/1299/ on March 29, 2017.

Fierros, E. G. (2006). One size does not fit all: A response to institutionalizing inequity. *Disability Studies Quarterly, 26*(2). Accessed at http://dsq-sds.org/article/view/683/860 on January 30, 2017.

Fisher, D., & Frey, N. (2016). Transfer goals for deeper learning. *Educational Leadership, 73*(6), 80–81.

Fisher, D., Frey, N., & Lapp, D. (2011). Coaching middle-level teachers to think aloud improves comprehension instruction and student reading achievement. *Teacher Educator, 46*(3), 231–243.

Flanagan, S. M., & Bouck, E. C. (2015). Mapping out the details: Supporting struggling writers' written expression with concept mapping. *Preventing School Failure, 59*(4), 244–252.

Flavell, J. H. (1976). Metacognitive aspects of problem solving. In L. B. Resnick (Ed.), *The nature of intelligence* (pp. 231–236). Hillsdale, NJ: Erlbaum.

Flixercise. (2012). *Adapted physical education.* Accessed at www.flixercise.com/system/files/adaptedPE.pdf on February 1, 2016.

Flocabulary. (2016). *Pythagorean theorem: Printable exercise preview.* Accessed at www.flocabulary.com/unit/pythagorean-theorem/printable-activity on February 6, 2017.

Florida Department of Education. (n.d.). *State literacy plan.* Accessed at www.fldoe.org/core/fileparse.php/7539/urlt/strivingreaders.pdf on February 27, 2017.

Foorman, B., Beyler, N., Borradaile, K., Coyne, M., Denton, C. A., Dimino, J., et al. (2016). *Foundational skills to support reading for understanding in kindergarten through 3rd grade: Educator's practice guide* (NCEE 2016–4008). Washington, DC: U.S. Department of Education, Institute of Education Sciences, National Center for Education Evaluation and Regional Assistance.

Franklin-Rohr, C. (2012). Differentiation and the twice-exceptional student. *Understanding Our Gifted, 24*(2), 25–27.

Gamm, S., Elliott, J., Halbert, J. W., Price-Baugh, R., Hall, R., Walston, D., et al. (2012). *Common Core State Standards and diverse urban students: Using multi-tiered systems of support.* Washington, DC: Council of Great City Schools.

Gansle, K. A., & Noell, G. H. (2007). The fundamental role of intervention implementation in assessing resistance to intervention. In S. Jimerson, M. K. Burns, & A. M. VanDerHeyden (Eds.), *Handbook of response to intervention: The science and practice of assessment and intervention* (pp. 244–254). New York: Springer.

Garbacz, S. A., Lannie, A. L., Jeffrey-Pearsall, J. L., & Truckenmiller, A. J. (2015). Strategies for effective classroom coaching. *Preventing School Failure, 59*(4), 263–273.

Gardner, H. (1995). Reflections on multiple intelligences: Myths and messages. *Phi Delta Kappan, 77*(3), 200–209.

Gersten, R., Compton, D., Connor, C. M., Dimino, J., Santoro, L., Linan-Thompson, S., et al. (2008). *Assisting students struggling with reading: Response to intervention (RtI) and multi-tier intervention in the primary grades—IES practice guide* (NCEE 2009–4045). Washington, DC: U.S. Department of Education, Institute of Education Sciences, National Center for Education Evaluation and Regional Assistance.

Gersten, R., Beckmann, S., Clarke, B., Foegen, A., Marsh, L., Star, J. R., et al. (2009). *Assisting students struggling with mathematics: Response to intervention (RtI) for elementary and middle schools* (NCEE 2009–4060). Washington, DC: U.S. Department of Education, Institute of Education Sciences, National Center for Education Evaluation and Regional Assistance.

Gersten, R., & Vaughn, S. (2009). *Evolution of response to intervention.* Accessed at https://ies.ed.gov /ncee/wwc/Docs/PracticeGuide/wwc_rrti_pg_chair06.pdf on March 16, 2016.

Gilles, R. (2016). Cooperative learning: Review of research and practice. *Australian Journal of Teacher Education, 41*(3), 39–54.

Global Reading Network. (n.d.). *EdData.* Accessed at www.eddataglobal.org/about/index.cfm on January 18, 2016.

Gongadze, N. (2011, October 19). *The Simpsons—Edgar Allan Poe: The Raven* [Video file]. Accessed at www.youtube.com/watch?v=bLiXjaPqSyY on October 18, 2016.

Gonzales, L., & Young, C. (2015). Delivering the 'WOW': Redesigning learning environments. *Educational Leadership, 45*(2), 28–32.

Graham, S., Bruch, J., Fitzgerald, J., Friedrich, L., Furgeson, J., Greene, K., et al. (2016). *Teaching secondary students to write effectively: Educator's practice guide* (NCEE 2017–4002). Washington, DC: U.S. Department of Education, Institute of Education Sciences, National Center for Education Evaluation and Regional Assistance. Accessed at https://ies.ed.gov/ncee/wwc/Docs /PracticeGuide/wwc_secondary_writing_110116.pdf on February 3, 2017.

Grimes, J., Kurns, S., & Tilly, W. D. (2006). Sustainability: An enduring commitment to success. *School Psychology Review, 35*(2), 224–244.

Guenther, L. (2016). *Tall tales: Paul Bunyan.* Accessed at www.kidzone.ws/creative-writing/tall-tales on October 12, 2016.

Guerin, A., & Murphy, B. (2015). Repeated reading as a method to improve reading fluency for struggling adolescent readers. *Journal of Adolescent and Adult Literacy, 58*(7), 551–560.

Guggenheim, D. (Executive Producer/Director). (2006). *An inconvenient truth* [Motion picture]. United States: Paramount.

Hall, T., Cohen, N., & Vue, G. (2015). Addressing learning disabilities with UDL and technology: Strategic reader. *Learning Disability Quarterly, 38*(2), 72–83.

Hallahan, D. P., Kauffman, J. M., & Pullen, P. C. (2015). *Exceptional learners: An introduction to special education* (13th ed.). Boston: Pearson.

Haring, N. G., Lovitt, T. C., Eaton, M. D., & Hansen, C. L. (1978). *The fourth R: Research in the classroom.* Columbus, OH: Merrill.

Harlacher, J. E., Potter, J. B., & Weber, J. M. (2015). A team-based approach to improve core instructional reading practices within response to intervention. *Intervention in School and Clinic, 50*(4), 210–220.

Hasni, A., & Potvin, P. (2015). Student's interest in science and technology and its relationships with teaching methods, family context and self-efficacy. *International Journal of Environment and Science Education, 10*(3), 337–366.

Heckman, J., Stixrud, J., & Urzua, S. (2006). The effects of cognitive and noncognitive abilities on labor market outcomes and social behavior. *Journal of Labor Economics, 24*(3), 411–482.

Hickman, R., & Kiss, L. (2010). Cross-curricular gallery learning: A phenomenological case study. *International Journal of Art and Design Education, 29*(1), 27–36.

Hierck, T., Coleman, C., & Weber, C. (2011). *Pyramid of behavior interventions: Seven keys to a positive learning environment.* Bloomington, IN: Solution Tree Press.

Hill, D. R., King, S. A., Lemons, C. J., & Partanen, J. N. (2012). Fidelity of implementation and instructional alignment in response to intervention research. *Learning Disabilities Research and Practice, 27*(3), 116–124.

Hinton, V., Flores, M. M., & Shippen, M. (2013). Response to intervention and math instruction. *International Journal of Education in Mathematics, Science and Technology, 1*(3), 190–201.

Hinton, V., Strozier, S. D., & Flores, M. M. (2014). Building mathematical fluency for students with disabilities or students at-risk for mathematics failure. *International Journal of Education in Mathematics, Science and Technology, 2*(4), 257–265.

History. (n.d.a). *Lead story: 1954—Brown v Board of Ed is decided* [Video file]. Accessed at www .history.com/this-day-in-history/brown-v-board-of-ed-is-decided on February 3, 2017.

History. (n.d.b). *U.S. immigration before 1965.* Accessed at www.history.com/topics/u-s-immigration -before-1965 on July 11, 2016.

Hoerr, T. R. (2016). Multiple ways to learn. *Educational Leadership, 73*(6), 86–87.

Huebner, T. A. (2010). Differentiated learning. *Educational Leadership, 67*(5), 79–81.

Hughes, B. (n.d.). *Lesson plan: Internalization of vocabulary through the use of a word map*. Accessed at www.readwritethink.org/classroom-resources/lesson-plans/internalization-vocabulary-through -word-307.html on February 3, 2017.

Hunter, W. C., Maheady, L., Jasper, A. D., Williamson, R. L., Murley, R. C., & Stratton, E. (2015). Numbered heads together as a Tier 1 instructional strategy in multitiered systems of support. *Education and Treatment of Children, 38*(3), 345–362.

Hutchinson, A. C., & Colwell, J. (2014). The potential of digital technologies to support literacy instruction relevant to the Common Core State Standards. *Journal of Adolescent and Adult Literacy, 58*(2), 147–156.

International Dyslexia Association. (2016). *Multisensory structured language teaching*. Accessed at https://eida.org/multisensory-structured-language-teaching on June 1, 2016.

International Literacy Association. (2009). IRA commission on RTI: Working draft of guiding principles. *Reading Today, 26*(4), 1–6.

International Literacy Association. (2010). *Response to intervention: Guiding principles for educators from the International Reading Association*. Newark, DE: Author.

Irvin, J. L., Meltzer, J., & Dukes, M. (2007). *Taking action on adolescent literacy: An implementation guide for school leaders*. Alexandria, VA: Association for Supervision and Curriculum Development.

Jacobs, H. (2012). Foreword. In H. F. Silver, R. T. Dewing, & M. J. Perini, *Core six: Essential strategies for achieving excellence with the Common Core* (pp. vii–viii). Alexandria, VA: Association for Supervision and Curriculum Development.

Jager, B., Reezigt, G. J., & Creemers, B. P. (2002). The effects of teacher training on new instructional behavior in reading comprehension. *Teaching and Teacher Education, 18*(7), 831–842.

Jetton, T. L., & Alexander, P. A. (2004). Domains, teaching, and literacy. In T. L. Jetton & J. A. Dole (Eds.), *Adolescent literacy research and practice* (pp. 15–39). New York: Guilford Press.

Jeyasekaran, J. M. (2015). Effectiveness of visual auditory kinesthetic tactile technique on reading level among children with dyslexia at Helikx Open School and Learning Centre, Salem. *International Journal of Medical Science and Public Health, 4*(3), 315–318.

Johnson, D. W., & Johnson, R. T. (n.d.). *An overview of cooperative learning*. Accessed at www.co -operation.org/what-is-cooperative-learning on June 3, 2016.

Jones, L. (2007). *The student-centered classroom*. New York: Cambridge University Press.

Jones, R. E., Yssel, N., & Grant, C. (2012). Reading instruction in Tier 1: Bridging the gaps by nesting evidence-based interventions within differentiated instruction. *Psychology in the Schools, 49*(3), 210–218.

Jose, G. R. (2015). Acquisition of vocabulary by dint of unique strategies: Indispensible for fostering English language skills. *Journal on English Language Teaching, 5*(2), 7–18.

Kamil, M. L., & Hiebert, E. H. (2005). Teaching and learning vocabulary: Perspectives and persistent issues. In E. H. Hiebert & M. L. Kamil (Eds.), *Teaching and learning vocabulary: Bringing research to practice* (pp. 1–23). Mahwah, NJ: Erlbaum.

Kanfush, P. M. (2014). Dishing direct instruction: Teachers and parents tell all! *Qualitative Report, 19*(1), 1–13.

Karten, T. J. (2010). *Inclusion lesson plan book for the 21st century.* Naples, FL: National Professional Resources.

Karten, T. J. (2011). *Inclusion strategies and interventions.* Bloomington, IN: Solution Tree Press.

Karten, T. J. (2012). *Inclusion lesson plan book for the 21st century* (Teacher training ed.). Naples, FL: National Professional Resources.

Karten, T. J. (2013). *Inclusion coaching for collaborative schools.* Thousand Oaks, CA: Corwin Press.

Karten, T. J. (2014). *IEPs and CCSS: Specially designed instructional strategies.* Naples, FL: National Professional Resources.

Karten, T. J. (2015). *Inclusion strategies that work! Research-based methods for the classroom* (3rd ed.). Thousand Oaks, CA: Corwin Press.

Kaufman, R. (2016). Harnessing the power of rigor and self-efficacy in the classroom. *Talent Development, 70*(3), 54–59.

Kayalar, F. (2016). Teachers' views over the workout strategies for helping students motivate themselves in the classroom. *Universal Journal of Educational Research, 4*(4), 868–877.

Kelly, K. (2014). *Visual-spatial processing issues: What you need to know.* Accessed at www.understood.org/en/learning-attention-issues/child-learning-disabilities/visual-processing-issues/visual-spatial-processing-what-you-need-to-know on October 12, 2016.

Khan, S. (n.d.). *Rewriting tricky fractions to decimals* [Video file]. Accessed at www.khanacademy.org/math/arithmetic-home/arith-review-decimals/decimals-to-fractions/v/converting-fractions-to-decimals on February 3, 2017.

Knight, J. (Ed.). (2009). *Coaching: Approaches and perspectives.* Thousand Oaks, CA: Corwin Press.

Knott, L., & Harding, M. (2014). *General prescribing guidance.* Accessed at http://patient.info/doctor/general-prescribing-guidance on July 12, 2016.

Kovaleski, J. F. (n.d.). *Teaching integrity protocols.* Accessed at www.rtinetwork.org/getstarted/evaluate/treatment-integrity-protocols on February 7, 2017.

Kretlow, A. G., & Bartholomew, C. C. (2010). Using coaching to improve the quality of evidence -based practices: A review of studies. *Teacher Education and Special Education, 33*(4), 279–299.

Kretlow, A. G., Wood, C. L., & Cooke, N. L. (2011). Using in-service and coaching to increase kindergarten teachers' accurate delivery of group instructional units. *Journal of Special Education, 44*(4), 234–246.

Learning Forward. (n.d.). *Standards for professional learning: Quick reference guide.* Accessed at http://learningforward.org/docs/pdf/standardsreferenceguide.pdf on January 5, 2016.

Learning Toolbox. (n.d.). *Cornell notes.* Accessed at http://coe.jmu.edu/learningtoolbox/cornellnotes .html on October 12, 2016.

Lee, H. (1960). *To kill a mockingbird.* Philadelphia: Lippincott.

Leko, M. M., & Brownell, M. T. (2009). Crafting quality professional development for special educators: What school leaders should know. *TEACHING Exceptional Children, 42*(1), 64–70.

Lenski, S. (2011). What RTI means for content area teachers. *Journal of Adolescent and Adult Literacy, 55*(4), 276–282.

Levinson, M. (2014, April 2). *4 tips to build student confidence* [Blog post]. Accessed at www.edutopia .org/blog/4-tips-build-student-confidence-matt-levinson on March 1, 2016.

Library of Congress. (n.d.a). *Immigration: Challenges for new Americans.* Accessed at www.loc.gov /teachers/classroommaterials/primarysourcesets/immigration on July 11, 2017.

Library of Congress. (n.d.b). *Teacher's guides and analysis tool.* Accessed at www.loc.gov/teachers /usingprimarysources/guides.html on February 3, 2017.

Library of Congress. (2010). *Spring 2010 teaching with primary sources quarterly learning activity: Secondary level—Understanding immigration through popular culture.* Accessed at www.loc.gov /teachers/tps/quarterly/pdf/Spring2010SecondaryLevelLearningActivity.pdf on July 11, 2016.

Lipson, M. Y., Chomsky-Higgins, P., & Kanfer, J. (2011). Diagnosis: The missing ingredient in RTI assessment. *The Reading Teacher, 65*(3), 204–208.

Lloyd, G. (2016). *The constitutional convention: Washington as statesman at the Constitutional Convention by Junius Brutus Stearns.* Accessed at http://teachingamericanhistory.org/convention/stearns on July 12, 2016.

Lord, C. (2006). *Rules.* New York: Scholastic.

Maiullo, J. (2016). Teaching techniques: Physical vocabulary in the beginner-level classroom. *English Teaching Forum, 54*(1), 31–34.

Malouf, R. C., Reisener, C. D., Gadke, D. L., Wimbish, S. W., & Frankel, A. C. (2014). The effect of helping early literacy with practice strategies on reading fluency for children with severe reading impairments. *Reading Improvement, 51*(2), 269–279.

Marcotte, A. M., & Hintze, J. M. (2009). Incremental and predictive utility of formative assessment methods of reading comprehension. *Journal of School Psychology, 47*(5), 315–335.

Margolis, H. (2012). Response to intervention: RTI's linchpins. *Reading Psychology, 33*(1), 8–10.

Marzano, R. J. (2007). *The art and science of teaching: A comprehensive framework for effective instruction.* Alexandria, VA: Association for Supervision and Curriculum Development.

Marzano, R. J., & Toth, M. D. (2014). *Teaching for rigor: A call for a critical instructional shift.* Accessed at www.marzanocenter.com/files/Teaching-for-Rigor-20140318.pdf on January 30, 2017.

Mathes, P. G., Denton, C. A., Fletcher, J. M., Anthony, J. L., Francis, D. J., & Schatschneider, C. (2005). The effects of theoretically different instruction and student characteristics on the skills of struggling readers. *Reading Research Quarterly, 40*(2), 148–182.

McCollough, S. (2014). *Student-centered classrooms promote the skills for lifelong learning.* Atlanta, GA: American Board for Certification of Teacher Excellence. Accessed at http://abcte.org/student-centered-classrooms-promote-the-skills-for-lifelong-learning-3114 on June 4, 2016.

McCormick, K. K. (2015). Making fractions meaningful. *Teaching Children Mathematics, 22*(4), 230–238.

McInerney, M., & Elledge, A. (2013). *Using a response to intervention framework to improve student learning: A pocket guide for state and district leaders—Implementing ESEA Flexibility Plans.* Indianapolis, IN: American Institutes for Research. Accessed at www.rti4success.org/sites/default/files/Response_to_Intervention_Pocket_Guide_2.pdf on June 29, 2016.

McKeone, A., Caruso, L., Bettle, K., Chase, A., Bryson, B., Schneider, J. S., et al. (2015). *Activities for challenging gifted learners by increasing complexity in the Common Core.* Accessed at http://files.eric.ed.gov/fulltext/ED556335.pdf on January 30, 2017.

McMaster, K. L., Parker, D., & Jung, P. G. (2012). Using curriculum-based measurement for beginning writers within a response to intervention framework. *Reading Psychology, 33*(1–2), 190–216.

Menzies, H. M, Mahdavi, J. N., & Lewis, J. L. (2008). Early intervention in reading: From research to practice. *Remedial and Special Education, 29*(2), 67–77.

Metcalf, T. (n.d.). *What's your plan? Accurate decision making within a multi-tier system of supports—Critical areas in Tier 1.* Accessed at www.rtinetwork.org/essential/tieredinstruction/tier1/accurate-decision-making-within-a-multi-tier-system-of-supports-critical-areas-in-tier-1 on May 27, 2016.

Meyer, M. M., & Behar-Horenstein, L. S. (2015). When leadership matters: Perspectives from a teacher team implementing response to intervention. *Education and Treatment of Children, 38*(3), 383–402.

Migration Policy Institute. (2014). *Largest U.S. immigration groups over time, 1960–present.* Accessed at www.migrationpolicy.org/programs/data-hub/charts/largest-immigrant-groups-over-time on July 11, 2016.

Ming, K. (2012). 10 content-area literacy strategies for art, mathematics, music, and physical education. *Clearing House: A Journal of Educational Strategies, Issues and Ideas, 85*(6), 213–220.

Montagu, A. (1966). *On being human.* New York: Hawthorne.

MooMooMath. (2015, March 3). *YouTube's top 10 fraction songs* [Blog post]. Accessed at www .moomoomathblog.com/2015/03/youtubes-top-10-fraction-songs.html on July 11, 2016.

Moore-Partin, T., Robertson, R. E., Maggin, D. M., Oliver, R. M., & Wehby, J. H. (2010). Using teacher praise and opportunities to respond to promote appropriate student behavior. *Preventing School Failure, 54*(3), 172–178.

Morgan, R. L., Menlove, R., Salzberg, C. L., & Hudson, P. (1994). Effects of peer coaching on the acquisition of direct instruction skills by low-performing preservice teachers. *Journal of Special Education, 28*(1), 59–76.

Morin, A. (n.d.). *Understanding ADHD.* Accessed at www.understood.org/en/learning-attention -issues/child-learning-disabilities/add-adhd/understanding-adhd on October 12, 2016.

Nast, P. (2014). *Teaching folklore.* Accessed at www.nea.org/tools/lessons/55635.htm on November 8, 2016.

National Assessment of Educational Progress. (2015). *2015 mathematics and reading assessments.* Accessed at www.nationsreportcard.gov/reading_math_2015/#?grade=4 on January 13, 2017.

National Association for Sport and Physical Education. (2000). *Appropriate instructional practice guidelines for elementary school physical education: A position statement from the National Association for Sport and Physical Education* (3rd ed.). Champaign, IL: Author.

National Center on Intensive Intervention at American Institutes for Research. (2014). *Phonics inventory.* Accessed at www.intensiveintervention.org/sites/default/files/Phonics_Inventory.pdf on December 30, 2015.

National Center on Response to Intervention. (n.d.). *Understanding types of assessment within an RTI framework.* Accessed at www.rti4success.org/sites/default/files/Understanding_Assessment _Transcript.pdf on November 8, 2016.

National Center on Response to Intervention. (2011). *RTI essential components integrity rubric.* Washington, DC: U.S. Department of Education, Office of Special Education Programs, National Center on Response to Intervention.

National Center on Universal Design for Learning. (2011). *Types of evidence supporting UDL.* Accessed at www.udlcenter.org/aboutudl/udlevidence on September 18, 2016.

National Center on Universal Design for Learning. (2014). *UDL guidelines: Version 2.0—Examples and resources.* Accessed at www.udlcenter.org/implementation/examples on September 19, 2016.

National Council of Teachers of English. (n.d.). *ReadWriteThink.* Accessed at www.readwritethink.org on January 31, 2017.

National Council of Teachers of Mathematics. (n.d.). *Times table.* Accessed at http://illuminations .nctm.org/Activity.aspx?id=4196 on January 10, 2016.

National Geographic. (n.d.). *What is global warming? The planet is heating up—And fast.* Accessed at http://environment.nationalgeographic.com/environment/global-warming/gw-overview.html on July 11, 2016.

National Geographic. (2016). *Global warming quiz.* Accessed at http://environment.nationalgeographic .com/environment/global-warming/quiz-global-warming/# on July 12, 2016.

National Institute for Direct Instruction. (n.d.). *Basic philosophy of direct instruction (DI).* Accessed at www.nifdi.org/what-is-di/basic-philosophy on July 11, 2016.

National Reading Panel. (2000). *Teaching children to read: An evidence-based assessment of the scientific research literature on reading and its implications for reading instruction.* Accessed at www.nichd.nih .gov/publications/pubs/nrp/documents/report.pdf on January 30, 2017.

Nelson, J. (2014). *The tree pose: Step-by-step instructions.* Accessed at www.yogajournal.com/pose/tree -pose on July 11, 2016.

New World Encyclopedia. (2013). *Lev Vygotsky.* Accessed at www.newworldencyclopedia.org/entry /Lev_Vygotsky on January 30, 2017.

Ning, H. K. (2016). Examining heterogeneity in student metacognition: A factor mixture analysis. *Learning and Individual Differences, 49,* 373–377.

Nobel Peace Laureate Project. (n.d.). *Theodore Roosevelt: 1906.* Accessed at www.nobelpeacelaureates .org/pdf/elem_TheodoreRoosevelt.pdf on January 30, 2017.

O'Connor, E., & Freeman, E. (2012). District-level considerations in supporting and sustaining RTI implementation. *Psychology in the Schools, 49*(3), 297–310.

O'Connor, R. E., & Klingner, J. (2010). Poor responders in RTI. *Theory Into Practice, 49*(4), 297–304.

Pallotta, J. (2002). *The Hershey's milk chocolate multiplication book.* New York: Scholastic.

Paulsen, G. (1987). *Hatchet.* New York: Simon & Schuster.

PE Central. (2015). *Differentiating instruction for students with disabilities.* Accessed at www.pecentral .org/adapted/adaptedactivities.html on February 5, 2016.

Perron, J., Gomez, A., & Testa, R. (2016). Harnessing the power of rigor and self-efficacy in the classroom. *Leadership, 46*(1), 8–10.

Poe, E. A. (1843). *The tell-tale heart.* Accessed at http://xroads.virginia.edu/~hyper/poe/telltale.html on July 11, 2016.

Poe, E. A. (1845). *The raven.* Accessed at www.poetryfoundation.org/poems-and-poets/poems/detail/48860 on July 12, 2016.

Poetry Soup. (2014). *Short flamingo poems.* Accessed at www.poetrysoup.com/poems/short/flamingo on July 11, 2016.

Pólya, G. (1957). *How to solve it: A new aspect of mathematical method* (2nd ed.). Princeton, NJ: Princeton University Press.

Public Broadcasting Service. (2007). *Alexander Hamilton: People and events—Creating the U.S. Constitution.* Accessed at www.pbs.org/wgbh/amex/hamilton/peopleevents/e_federalist.html on July 12, 2016.

Public Broadcasting Service. (2015). *For educators: Lesson plan index—Immigration policy past and present.* Accessed at www.pbs.org/independentlens/newamericans/foreducators_lesson_plan_03.html on July 11, 2016.

Rapp, J. T., Marvin, K. L., Nystedt, A., Swanson, G. J., Paananen, L., & Tabatt, J. (2012). Response repetition as an error-correction procedure for acquisition of math facts and math computation. *Behavioral Interventions, 27*(1), 16–32.

Rappaport, N., & Minahan, J. (2012). Cracking the behavior code. *Educational Leadership, 70*(2), 18–25.

Rasinski, T. V., Rupley, W. H., Paige, D. D., & Nichols, W. D. (2016). Alternative text types to improve reading fluency for competent to struggling readers. *International Journal of Instruction, 9*(1), 163–178.

Reading Rockets. (n.d.). *Reciprocal teaching.* Accessed at www.readingrockets.org/strategies/reciprocal_teaching on July 12, 2016.

ReadWriteThink. (2012). *Theme poems.* Accessed at www.readwritethink.org/files/resources/interactives/theme_poems on July 12, 2016.

ReadWorks. (2015). *Long live the vikings.* Accessed at www.readworks.org/passages/long-live-vikings on July 12, 2016.

Reid, R., Hagaman, J. L., & Graham, S. (2014). Using self-regulated strategy development for written expression with students with attention deficit hyperactivity disorder. *Learning Disabilities: A Contemporary Journal, 12*(1), 21–42.

Reinke, W. M., Herman, K. C., & Stormont, M. (2013). Classroom-level positive behavior supports in schools implementing SW-PBIS: Identifying areas for enhancement. *Journal of Positive Behavior Interventions, 15*(1), 39–50.

Richards, L. C., Heathfield, L. T., & Jenson, W. R. (2010). A classwide peer-modeling intervention package to increase on-task behavior. *Psychology in the Schools*, *47*(6), 551–566.

Rickabaugh, J. (2015). Including the learner in personalized learning. *Connect: Making Learning Personal—An issue brief from the League of Innovators*. Accessed at http://files.eric.ed.gov/fulltext/ED558048.pdf on February 6, 2017.

Riester-Wood, T. (2015). *Peers supporting an inclusive school climate*. Accessed at http://inclusiveschools.org/peers-supporting-an-inclusive-school-climate on June 3, 2016.

Rimbey, M., McKeown, M., Beck, I., & Sanora, C. (2016). Supporting teachers to implement contextualized and interactive practices in vocabulary instruction. *Journal of Education*, *196*(2), 69–87.

Robb, E., Sinatra, R., & Eschenauer, R. (2014). Vocabulary theatre: A peer-teaching approach for academic vocabulary acquisition. *Journal of Education and Training Studies*, *2*(1), 117–126.

Robins, J., & Antrim, P. (2013). Planning for RtI. *Knowledge Quest*, *42*(1), 44–47.

Robinson, K., & Aronica, L. (2015). *Creative schools: The grassroots revolution that's transforming education*. New York: Viking Press.

Rock, M. L., Gregg, M., Ellis, E., & Gable, R. A. (2008). REACH: A framework for differentiating classroom instruction. *Preventing School Failure*, *52*(2), 31–47.

Rosen, P. (2016). *Orton–Gillingham: What you need to know*. Accessed at www.understood.org/en/school-learning/partnering-with-childs-school/instructional-strategies/orton-gillingham-what-you-need-to-know on October 13, 2016.

Roy, G., Fueyo, V., Knudsen, J., Rafanan, K., & Lara-Meloy, T. (2016). Connecting representations: Using predict, check, explain. *Mathematics Teaching in the Middle School*, *21*(8), 492–496.

Rubinstein-Avila, E. (2013). Scaffolding content and language demands for "reclassified" students. *Voices From the Middle*, *20*(4), 28–33.

Rudd, L. C., Lambert, M. C., Satterwhite, M., & Smith, C. H. (2009). Professional development + coaching = enhanced teaching: Increasing usage of math mediated language in preschool classrooms. *Journal of Early Childhood Education*, *37*(1), 63–69.

Salem State College. (n.d.). *Document-based questions (DBQs): Fugitive Slave Act visual texts*. Accessed at http://landmark.salemstate.edu/fugitive_visual_texts.html on October 12, 2016.

Sanford, A. K., Harlacher, J. E., & Walker, N. J. N. (2010). The "I" in RTI: Research-based factors for intensifying instruction. *TEACHING Exceptional Children*, *42*(6), 30–38.

Sarason, S. B. (1996). *Revisiting "the culture of school and the problem of change."* New York: Teachers College Press.

Scanlon, D. M. (2013). Assessing RTI strategies: The trouble with packaged and scripted interventions. *Reading Today*, *31*(1), 20–21.

Schnorr, C. I. (2013). *Effects of multilevel support on first-grade teachers' use of research-based strategies during beginning reading instruction.* Unpublished doctoral dissertation, University of North Carolina at Charlotte.

Schoenbach, R., Greenleaf, C. L., & Hale, G. (2010). Framework fuels the need to read: Strategies boost literacy of students in content-area classes. *Journal of Staff Development*, *31*(5), 38–42.

Science Kids. (2016). *Animal facts: Fun flamingo facts for kids.* Accessed at www.sciencekids.co.nz /sciencefacts/animals/flamingo.html on July 11, 2016.

Scriven, M. (1991). *Evaluation thesaurus* (4th ed.). Thousand Oaks, CA: SAGE.

Searle, M. (2010). *What every school leader needs to know about RTI.* Alexandria, VA: Association for Supervision and Curriculum Development.

sheeberi. (2009). *When two vowels go walking* [Video file]. Accessed at www.youtube.com/watch ?v=o84ndBQU6vQ on February 3, 2017.

Shih, Y.-C., & Reynolds, B. L. (2015). Teaching adolescents EFL by integrating think-pair-share and reading strategy instruction: A quasi-experimental study. *Journal of Language Teaching and Research*, *46*(3), 221–235.

Shoemaker, C. A. (2010). Student confidence as a measure of learning in an undergraduate principles of horticultural science course. *HortTechnology*, *20*(4), 683–688.

Sieberer-Nagler, K. (2016). Effective classroom-management & positive teaching. *English Language Teaching*, *9*(1),163–172.

Silver, H. F., Dewing, R. T., & Perini, M. J. (2012). *Core six: Essential strategies for achieving excellence with the Common Core.* Alexandria, VA: Association for Supervision and Curriculum Development.

Siri, D. K., Zinner, J., & Lezin, N. (2011). Blending rigor and relevance. *Leadership*, *40*(3), 8–11.

Slavin, R. E. (2014). Making cooperative learning powerful. *Educational Leadership*, *72*(2), 22–26.

Society of Health and Physical Educators America. (2009). *Appropriate instructional practice guidelines, K–12: A side-by-side comparison.* Accessed at www.shapeamerica.org/standards/guidelines/upload /Appropriate-Instructional-Practices-Grid.pdf on March 12, 2016.

Soto, I., & Calderón, M. E. (2016). *Academic language mastery: Vocabulary in context.* Thousand Oaks, CA: Corwin Press.

Sprenger, M. (2013). *Teaching the critical vocabulary of the Common Core: 55 words that make or break student understanding.* Alexandria, VA: Association for Supervision and Curriculum Development.

Stankov, L., Morony, S., & Lee, Y. P. (2014). Confidence: The best non-cognitive predictor of academic achievement? *Educational Psychology, 34*(1), 9–28.

Stecker, P. M. (n.d.). *Monitoring student progress in individualized educational programs using curriculum -based measurement.* Washington, DC: National Center on Student Progress Monitoring. Accessed at www.studentprogress.org/library/monitoring_student_progress_in_individualized_educational _programs_using_cbm.pdf on May 30, 2016.

Sternberg, R. J. (2000). Patterns of giftedness: A triarchic analysis. *Roeper Review, 22*(4), 231–235.

Sternberg, R. J. (2014). The current status of the theory of structural cognitive modifiability in relation to theories of intelligence. *Transylvanian Journal of Psychology,* 9–13.

Sugai, G. (2016). *MTSS/PBIS and educational excellence: The blueprint for educational excellence conference* [PowerPoint slides]. Accessed at www.pbis.org/Common/Cms/files/pbisresources/12%20 Apr%20MTSS%20PBIS%20gsugai%20HAND.pdf on June 2, 2016.

Sumantri, M. S., & Satriani, R. (2016). The effect of formative testing and self-directed learning on mathematics learning outcomes. *International Electronic Journal of Elementary Education, 8*(3), 507–524.

Tanner, K. D. (2012). Promoting student metacognition. *CBE Life Science Education, 11*(2), 113–120. Accessed at www.ncbi.nlm.nih.gov/pmc/articles/PMC3366894 on October 13, 2016.

Tatum, A. W. (2011). Diversity and literacy. In S. J. Samuels & A. E. Farstrup (Eds.), *What research has to say about reading instructio*n (4th ed., pp. 425–447). Newark, DE: International Literacy Association.

TeachersFirst. (n.d.). *The raven: An interactive study resource.* Accessed at http://teachersfirst.com/lessons /raven/start-fl.cfm on October 13, 2016.

Teaching Channel. (n.d.). *Introduction to trigonometry: Grade 8/math/triangles* [Video file]. Accessed at www.teachingchannel.org/videos/introduction-to-trigonometry on February 6, 2017.

Teachinghistory.org. (2016). *Using document-based questions with struggling readers.* Accessed at http://teachinghistory.org/teaching-materials/ask-a-master-teacher/14958 on October 13, 2016.

Teaching Tolerance. (n.d.). *Immigration myths.* Accessed at www.tolerance.org/lesson/immigration-myths on February 6, 2017.

Templeton, S. (2015). Building foundational and vocabulary knowledge in the Common Core, K–8: Developmentally-grounded instruction about words. *Language and Literacy Spectrum, 25,* 7–17.

Thompson, A. (2009, September 17). Why flamingos stand on one leg. *LiveScience.* Accessed at www .livescience.com/5732-flamingos-stand-leg.html on July 11, 2016.

Thoughtful Learning. (2016). *What are literacy skills?* Accessed at https://k12.thoughtfullearning.com /FAQ/what-are-literacy-skills on January 10, 2016.

Tomlinson, C. A. (2016). Mileposts of a meaningful life. *Educational Leadership*, *73*(6), 88–89.

Tomlinson, C. A. (1999). Leadership for differentiated classrooms. *School Administrator*, *56*(9), 6–11.

Torgesen, J. K., Houston, D. D., Rissman, L. M., Decker, S. M., Roberts, G., Vaughn, S., et al. (2007). *Academic literacy instruction for adolescents: A guidance document from the Center on Instruction.* Portsmouth, NH: RMC Research Corporation, Center on Instruction.

Turse, K. A., & Albrecht, S. F. (2015). The ABCs of RTI: An introduction to the building blocks of response to intervention. *Preventing School Failure*, *59*(2), 83–89.

University of Illinois at Urbana-Champaign, University Library. (2015). *Tips on writing learning outcomes.* Accessed at www.library.illinois.edu/infolit/learningoutcomes.html on June 1, 2016.

University of Nebraska-Lincoln, College of Education and Human Sciences. (2016). *Teaching strategies.* Accessed at http://cehs.unl.edu/secd/teaching-strategies on February 14, 2016.

University of South Florida, Florida's Positive Behavior Support Project. (2016). *MTSS implementation components: Ensuring common language and understanding.* Tampa, FL: Author. Accessed at www .florida-rti.org/educatorResources/MTSS_Book_ImplComp_012612.pdf on October 13, 2016.

University of South Florida, Problem Solving and Response to Intervention Project. (2016). *MTSS: A multi-tiered system of supports—Problem solving and response to intervention.* Tampa, FL: Author. Accessed at http://floridarti.usf.edu/floridaproject/mtss.html on October 13, 2016.

U.S. Department of Education, Institute of Education Sciences, National Center for Education Evaluation and Regional Assistance. (2003). *Identifying and implementing educational practices supported by rigorous evidence: A user-friendly guide.* Accessed at www2.ed.gov/rschstat/research /pubs/rigorousevid/index.html on October 13, 2016.

Utley, C. A., & Obiakor, F. E. (2015). Special issue: Research perspectives on multi-tiered system of support. *Learning Disabilities: A Contemporary Journal*, *13*(1), 1–2.

Vacca, R. T., Vacca, J. L., & Mraz, M. E. (2010). *Content area reading: Literacy and learning across the curriculum* (10th ed.). Boston: Pearson.

Vander Ark, T., & Schneider, C. (2014). *Deeper learning for every student every day: Executive summary.* Accessed at www.gettingsmart.com/publication/deeper-learning-every-student-every-day/ on October 27, 2016.

VanDerHeyden, A., & Allsopp, D. (2014). *Innovation configuration for mathematics* (Document No. IC-6). Gainesville: University of Florida, Collaboration for Effective Educator, Development, Accountability, and Reform Center. Accessed at http://ceedar.education.ufl.edu/wp-content /uploads/2014/09/IC-6_FINAL_09-25-14.pdf on January 30, 2017.

Vygotsky, L. S. (1978). *Mind in society: The development of higher psychological processes.* Cambridge, MA: Harvard University Press.

Walsh, K., Glaser, D., & Wilcox, D. D. (2006). *What elementary schools aren't teaching about reading and what elementary teachers aren't learning.* Washington, DC: National Council on Teacher Quality. Accessed at www.nctq.org/dmsView/What_Ed_Schools_Arent_Teaching_About_Reading_NCTQ _Report on January 30, 2017.

Wangru, C. (2016). Vocabulary teaching based on semantic-field. *Journal of Education and Learning, 5*(3), 64–71.

Wass, R., & Golding, C. (2014). Sharpening a tool for teaching: The zone of proximal development. *Teaching in Higher Education, 19*(6), 671–684.

Watts-Taffe, S., Laster, B. P., Broach, L., Marinak, B., Connor, C. M., & Walker-Dalhouse, D. (2012). Differentiated instruction: Making informed teacher decisions. *The Reading Teacher, 66*(4), 303–314.

Wehman, P. (Ed.). (2013). *Life beyond the classroom: Transition strategies for young people with disabilities* (5th ed.). Baltimore: Brookes.

Weida, S., & Stolley, K. (2013). *Using research and evidence.* Accessed at https://owl.english.purdue.edu /owl/resource/588/02 on October 13, 2016.

Werts, M. G., Lambert, M., & Carpenter, E. (2009). What special education directors say about RTI. *Learning Disability Quarterly, 32*(4), 245–254.

Wiggins, G. (2010). *What is a big idea?* Accessed at www.authenticeducation.org/ae_bigideas/article .lasso?artid=99 on January 7, 2016.

Wiggins, G., & McTighe, J. (2011). *The understanding by design guide to creating high-quality units.* Alexandria, VA: Association for Supervision and Curriculum Development.

Williams, R. B. (2002). *Multiple intelligences for differentiated learning.* Thousand Oaks, CA: Corwin Press.

Willis, J. (2006). *Research-based strategies to ignite student learning: Insights from a neurologist and classroom teacher.* Alexandria, VA: Association for Supervision and Curriculum Development.

Wixson, K. K., & Valencia, S. W. (2011). Assessment in RTI: What teachers and specialists need to know. *The Reading Teacher, 64*(6), 466–469.

Wood, C. L., Goodnight, C. I., Bethune, K. S., Preston, A. I., & Cleaver, S. L. (2016). Role of professional development and multi-level coaching in promoting evidence-based practice in education. *Learning Disabilities, 14*(2), 159–170.

Wright, J. (2013a). *Best practices in secondary math interventions (7–12).* Accessed at www .interventioncentral.org/wi_ed_math on March 5, 2016.

Wright, J. (2013b). *How to: Use the instructional hierarchy to identify effective teaching and intervention targets.* Accessed at www.jimwrightonline.com/mixed_files/lansing_IL/_Lansing_IL_Aug_2013/5 _instructional_hierarchy_revised.pdf on October 13, 2016.

Yale Center for Dyslexia and Creativity. (n.d.). *An index of successful dyslexics.* Accessed at http://bit.ly /2n7Z9kp on March 15, 2017.

Yeagar, D. S., & Dweck, C. S. (2012). Mindsets that promote resilience: When students believe that personal characteristics can be developed. *Educational Psychologist, 47*(4), 302–314.

Yoon, G., & Vargas, P. (2014). Know thy avatar: The unintended effect of virtual-self representation on behavior. *Psychological Science, 25*(4), 1043–1045.

Yoon, K. S., Duncan, T., Lee, S. W.-Y., Scarloss, B., & Shapley, K. L. (2007). *Reviewing the evidence on how teacher professional development affects student achievement: Summary* (Issues & Answers Report, REL 2007-003). Washington, DC: U.S. Department of Education, Institute of Education Sciences, National Center for Education Evaluation and Regional Assistance, Regional Educational Laboratory Southwest. Accessed at https://ies.ed.gov/ncee/edlabs/regions/southwest/pdf/REL _2007033_sum.pdf on January 30, 2017.

Zepeda, C. D., Richey, J. E., Ronevich, P., & Nokes-Malach, T. J. (2015). Direct instruction of metacognition benefits adolescent science learning, transfer, and motivation: An in vivo study. *Journal of Educational Psychology, 107*(4), 954–970.

Zhao, Y. (2012). *World class learners: Educating creative and entrepreneurial students.* Thousand Oaks, CA: Corwin Press.

INDEX

A

academic achievements, support for, 100

academic language. *See* vocabulary

academic levels, diversity and, 41

academic literacy, 22, 68

Academy of Orton-Gillingham Practitioners and Educators, 103

access, certain, 4

accommodations, 67–68

administrators, support from, 138–139

AIMSweb System Review, 77

assessments

convergent, 4

data, 76–78

diagnostic, 76

formative, 46, 76–77

rating, 45–46

role of accurate, 11–12

summative, 77–78

tools for literacy and language arts, 46–48

Assisting Students Struggling With Reading: Response to Intervention (RtI) and Multi-Tier Intervention in the Primary Grades (Gersten), 46–47

automaticity, 32, 43, 44, 48, 57–58, 69, 121, 126, 128, 129

A–Z Vocabulary List, 29, 37

B

Behar-Horenstein, L., 135

behavioral interventions, 74–76, 100–109

behavioral screening tools, 49–50

Behavior Rating Inventory of Executive Functions, 49

behaviors, list of appropriate versus inappropriate, 102

Bender, W., 11

Benson, J., 128

big ideas (best practices)

interventions, accommodations, and modifications, 67–68

literacy and mathematics achievements, 66–67

Buffum, A., 2, 4, 13, 15, 74, 136

C

Center on Response to Intervention at American Institutes for Research, The, 45, 46

certain access, 4

Chace, W. M., 42

Charles, R. I., 66

Children's Depression Inventory, 49

Cisneros, S., 100

ClassDojo, 104

classroom dynamics, 10–11

classroom expository, 99

coaching, 138

cognitive strategy instruction (CSI), 121

Coleman, C., 101

collaboration, 99–100, 137, 144

collective responsibility, 4

Comprehension of Fiction, Narrative, and Expository Text, 23, 36

concentrated instruction, 4

Conners Comprehensive Behavior Rating Scales, 49

content-area literacy, 67

contextually engaging tasks, 14

convergent assessment, 4

cooperative learning, 122–124

core knowledge, 5, 6, 7, 11, 53, 57, 58, 69

Council for Exceptional Children, 39

Csikszentmihalyi, M., 120

curriculum-based measurement, 77

Curriculum Dice Game, 80, 83, 95

curriculum entry points. *See* multiple curriculum entry points

Cushing, H., 143

D

Developmental Reading Assessment (DRA), 47, 77

Dewing, T., 5

diagnostic assessments, 76

differentiated instruction, 1, 12, 50–51

direct instruction, 122

disabilities, 121–122

diversity. *See* spectrum

Dynamic Indicators of Basic Early Literacy Skills (DIBELS), 77

dyslexia, 103, 143

E

early literacy skills, assessing, 22–23

EasyCBM, 77

Edison, T., 143

elementary class science scenario, 104–106

Eleven (Cisneros), 100

engagements, 5–6
    fine-tune and individualize, 120
    minimizing and maximizing, 114–115
    pace, repeat, and enrich, 116–119
    planning, 113–129

evaluations. *See* assessments

evidence-based practice, 5–6
    academic and behavioral support, 100–102
    big ideas (best practices), 69–78
    cohesive framework, 12
    contextually engaging tasks, 14
    planning engagements for rigorous learning, 120–124
    prescriptive and responsive instruction, 12–13
    spectrum (diversity), 44–52
    vocabulary, 22–23

exceptionality, 121

explicit instruction, 3

F

fidelity. *See* professional development (fidelity)

First Steps in Mathematics, 48

First Steps Writing Map of Development, 48

Flocabulary, 14

formative assessments, 46, 76–77

four Cs of RTI, 4

Functional Analysis Screening Tool, 49

G

Gardner, H., 99

Bill and Melinda Gates Foundation, 41

Gersten, R., 46–47, 48

Glover, D., 143

Goldberg, W., 143

grades 2–3 language arts lesson on *Frozen*, 53–54

grade 3 lesson on Viking culture, 25–27

grade 5 literacy lesson on *Hatchet*, 79–80, 81

grade 5 long-range monthly lesson plans, 117, 118–119, 133

grade 5 quarterly lesson plans, 117–118, 132

grade 7 interdisciplinary lesson, 81

grade 7 language arts lesson on "The Raven," 54–55

grade 8 vocabulary lesson on the Federalists, 27–29

grade 9 English monthly lesson plans, 119

grade 10 American history lesson on African American history, 56–57

grade 10 immigration informational article lesson, 82–83

grade 10 vocabulary lesson on global warming, 30–31

graphic organizers, use of, 25, 26, 27

Greider, C., 143

Group Reading Assessment and Diagnostic Evaluation, 76

H

Hallahan, D., 3

Hierck, T., 101

high school geometry class scenario, 107–109

Hintze, J. M., 46

Hoerr, T. R., 99

I

Inclusion Lesson Plan Book for the 21st Century (Karten), 117

Individuals With Disabilities Education Act (IDEA), 121–122

instruction
    concentrated, 4
    direct, 122
    prescriptive and responsive, 12–13

Instructional Practice Guidelines for Middle School Physical Education, 106

intelligence(s)
    analytic, 121
    practical, 121
    synthetic, 121
    theory of multiple, 99
    triarchic theory of, 99, 121–122

interests, diversity and, 41–43

Interests and Strengths Questionnaire, 42, 59

J

Jacobs, H. H., 5

Jones, L., 15

Jose, G. R., 17

just-in-case scenarios, 74

K

Karten, T. J., 117

Kauffman, J., 3

KeyMath-3, 48, 76

Khan, S., 50, 103

Khan Academy, 109

Klinger, J., 4

knowledge
    core, 5
    interests and, 42

KWL charts, use of, 25, 26, 115–116, 121, 131

L

leadership, 136

learner outcomes, 80, 84

learner variability, respect for, 98–100

learning
  cooperative, 122–124
  environments, 73–74
  planning rigorous, 113–129

Lesson-Planning Template: Learner Outcomes and Skills, 58, 62–63

Lesson-Planning Template: Lessons Across the Disciplines, 78, 84, 94

lesson plans
  monthly, 117, 118–119, 133
  pace, repeat, and enrich, 116–119
  quarterly, 117–118, 132

listening comprehension, 14

literacy
  content-area, 67
  defined, 66–67
  scenario, 15–16

literacy and language arts, screening tools for, 46–48

M

Marcotte, A. M., 46

mathematical computations and applications, 14, 127–129

mathematics
  achievements, 66–67
  scenario, 16
  screening tools for, 48–49

Math Reasoning Inventory (MRI), 48

Mattos, M., 2, 74

McTighe, J., 57

Meyer, M., 135

middle school class physical education scenario, 106–107

mindsets, 15

modifications, 67, 68

motivation, 43–44

multiple curriculum entry points, 6
  academic and behavioral support, 103–109
  big ideas (best practices), 78–84
  mindsets and strategies, 15
  planning engagements for rigorous learning, 124–129
  spectrum (diversity), 52–58
  vocabulary, 23–33

multitiered system of supports (MTSS), 1
  response to intervention and, 44–50
  role of, 69

multitiered system of supports lesson connections, 15–16
  academic and behavioral support, 104–109
  big ideas (best practices), 78–84
  spectrum (diversity), 52–57
  vocabulary, 25–33

My Behavior Chart, 102, 111

N

National Center on Response to Intervention, The, 76

National Council of Teachers of English (NCTE), 25

National Reading Technical Assistance Center, 22

O

O'Connor, R., 4

O'Leary, K., 143

oral expression, 14

overlearning, 57–58

oxygen supplier, 42

P

Parts of a Book, 68, 86

peer supports, 124

People, Places, and Things Chart, 68, 89

Perini, M., 5

Phelps, M., 143

phonemic awareness and fluency
    description of, in tiers, 125–122
    record for, 23, 35

Pólya, G., 99, 104

Positive Behavioral Interventions and Supports (PBIS), 49, 101–102

POW-TREE strategy, 72

Problem-Solving Approach: Turning Challenge Into Growth, 109, 112

problem-solving approaches, 99–100

professional development (fidelity)
    checklists, 137
    parameters for, 139–140, 141
    preparation and sustainability, 139–140
    role of, 136–139

PRO-vocabulary instruction, 31–33, 38

Pullen, P., 3

Q

Qualitative Reading Inventory, 76

R

reading
    comprehension, 14, 71–72, 126–127
    fluency, 14
    strategic, 70–73

Reading Reflection Chart, 72, 92

real-world connections, 124–129

Record of Mathematics Skills, Concepts, and Engagements, 68, 90

Record of Student Participation, 69, 91

Reid, R., 72

Research Institute on Progress Monitoring, 77

response to intervention (RTI)
    contextually engaging tasks, 14
    defined, 1
    four Cs of, 4
    framework, 12
    inverted pyramid, 2, 13
    mindsets and strategies, 15
    multitiered system of supports and, 44–50
    prescriptive and responsive instruction, 12–13
    traditional pyramid, 2
    variables, 9–17

responsibility, collective, 4

rigorous learning, planning, 113–129

Roosevelt, T., 42

RTI. See response to intervention

RTI Action Network, 137

S

SAT, 77

Scholastic Math Inventory, 48

Schwab, C., 143

screening. See assessments

side-by-side coaching, 138

Silver, H., 5

Slavin, R. E., 123

spectrum
    academic levels, 41
    interests, 41–43
    motivation, 43–44
    respect for learner variability, 98–100

Spencer, H., 15

Stake, R., 77–78

State of Texas Assessments of Academic Readiness (STAAR), 45, 77

Sternberg, R. J., 99, 121

strategy table, 74

Student-Centered Classroom, The (Jones), 15

student-specific tiers, 98

summative assessments, 77–78

supervisory coaching, 138

sustainability, 139–140

Syllable Types, 68, 87

systematic instruction, 3

T

takeaways from lessons, 41

task analysis, 52

Tatum, A. W., 121

teacher expertise, 11–12

Teachers College Reading and Writing Project, 48

technology, use of, 50

Texas Primary Reading Inventory, 47–48

Tiered UDL-MTSS Literacy Planner, 53, 60–61

Tier 1 (primary) instruction (intervention)
  behavioral interventions, 75–76
  description of, 2, 3, 12, 44–45
  geometry instruction, 108
  mathematical computations and applications, 128–129
  phonemic awareness and fluency, 126
  physical education instruction and modeling, 106–107
  reading comprehension, 127
  visuals, use of, 105

Tier 1 vocabulary, 20

Tier 2 (secondary) instruction (intervention)
  behavioral interventions, 76
  description of, 2, 3–4, 12, 13, 44–45
  geometry instruction, 108

learning environment, 73
  mathematical computations and applications, 128, 129
  multisensory activities, 105
  phonemic awareness and fluency, 126
  physical education multitiered engagements, 107
  reading comprehension, 127
  student learning at, view of, 137
  student-specific, 98
  visual, auditory, and kinesthetic/tactical approaches, 103

Tier 2 vocabulary, 20

Tier 3 (tertiary) instruction (intervention)
  behavioral interventions, 76
  decoding scaffolds, 105
  description of, 2, 4, 12, 13, 44–45
  geometry instruction, 108
  learning environment, 73
  mathematical computations and applications, 128, 129
  phonemic awareness and fluency, 126
  physical education personalized feedback, 107
  reading comprehension, 127
  student learning at, view of, 138
  student-specific, 98
  visual, auditory, and kinesthetic/tactical approaches, 103

Tier 3 vocabulary, 20

Tomlinson, C. A., 125

TREE strategy, 72

triarchic theory of intelligence, 99, 121–122

U

universal design for learning (UDL), 1, 5, 51–52, 74

V

variables, 9–17

visual, auditory, and kinesthetic/tactical (VAKT) approaches, 103–104

vocabulary

academic literacy, 22, 68

development, 14

early literacy skills, assessing, 22–23

identifying, for instruction, 20–21

internalization, ensuring, 25

interventions, selecting, 21–22, 24–25

lesson connections, 25–33

PRO-vocabulary instruction, 31–33

student levels, determining, 21

tests, websites on, 21

tiers in, 20

word-identification levels, identifying, 24

Vygotsky, L., 40

W

Weber, C., 2, 74, 101

Wiggins, G., 57, 66

Willis, J., 31

Winkler, H., 143

Woodcock Reading Mastery, 47–48

word decoding, 71

word-identification levels, identifying, 24

Words and Questions Chart, 68, 88

writing fluency, 70–73

written expression, 14, 72–73

Written Expression Chart, 73, 93

Z

zone of proximal development, 40, 120

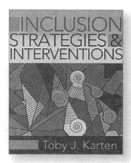

Inclusion Strategies & Interventions
Toby J. Karten

Inclusion means more than just preparing students to pass standardized tests and increasing academic levels. In inclusive classrooms, students with special educational needs are treated as integral members of the general education environment. Gain strategies to offer the academic, social, emotional, and behavioral benefits that allow all students to achieve their highest potential.
BKF381

Best Practices at Tier 1 series
Gayle Gregory, Martha Kaufeldt, and Mike Mattos

Improve core instruction to ensure learning for all. Created for K–12 educators, this series provides proven response to intervention strategies to differentiate instruction, engage students, increase success, and prevent additional interventions. Discover how to identify essential power standards to include in Tier 1 instruction, create a brain-friendly learning environment, shift instructional processes to support collaboration, and more.
BKF650, BKF651

It's About TIME series
Edited by Austin Buffum and Mike Mattos
Foreword by Rebecca DuFour and Richard DuFour

Carve out effective intervention and extension time at all three tiers of the RTI pyramid. Explore more than a dozen examples of creative and flexible scheduling, and gain access to tools you can use immediately to overcome implementation challenges. These books are full of examples from real schools that have achieved these results without using additional resources or extending the school day.
BKF609, BKF610

Developing Effective Learners
Toby J. Karten

Proactively address your students' diverse needs, using multitiered systems of support and response to intervention (RTI). The author details how to impactfully respond to students' academic, emotional, and behavioral challenges; embrace learning differences; and create inclusive classroom environments. Throughout the book, readers are supplied with tiered lessons, practical resources, instructional and staff scenarios, student vignettes, and responsive evidence-based interventions.
BKF734

The RTI Toolkit

Whether you're just beginning to build or working to fine-tune a system of intervention, this collection of resources guarantees to extend your knowledge even further. Learn how to control the intensity of the interventions while addressing learning gaps and meeting the needs of individual students. Loaded with dynamic strategies, this toolkit will keep your school culture healthy for years to come.
KTF133

"

WOW!

I liked how I was given an effective, organized plan to help EVERY child."

—Linda Rossiter, teacher,
Spring Creek Elementary School, Utah

PD Services

Our experts draw from decades of research and their own experiences to bring you practical strategies for providing timely, targeted interventions. You can choose from a range of customizable services, from a one-day overview to a multiyear process.

Book your RTI PD today!
888.763.9045

Solution Tree